CH00662660

To L & C,

For taking me on the greatest adventure of all

CONTENTS

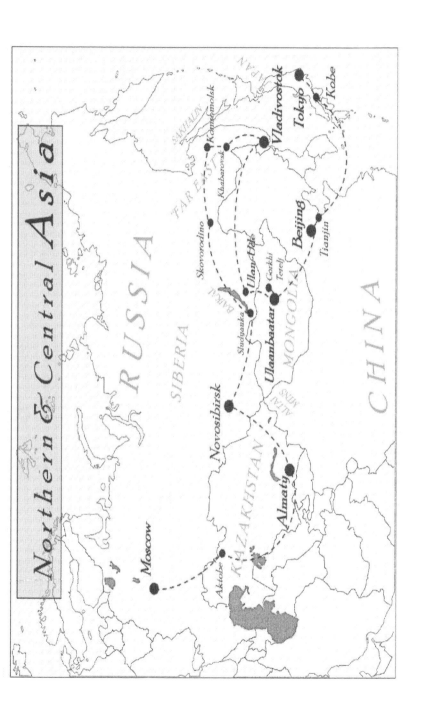

Northern & Central Asia

PROLOGUE

About a month before leaving Japan and embarking on this trip, I had given up a city job with a Tokyo Corporation. I was on the brink of a well-timed promotion and was even offered re-location to Osaka, to a position with more of a challenge. I was deep-seated and quite comfortable in this country, in this city, this beacon of the east. But I had to go. My colleagues did their best in encouraging me to stay, and said I might be turning my back on a good thing. I also had large reservations about going home to the UK after this length of time – the job market there was uncertain and I did like the pace of life in Tokyo, my friends, and my local community. I was a well-groomed city boy, living in a well-groomed Tokyo suburb. From my front door in west Tokyo, to the journey along the urban alleyways and swanky boulevards on my way to work, right up to exiting the lift onto the polished floors of my office, life certainly looked good from the outside. But I couldn't help but feel dissatisfied. This part of the world was amazing, but I hadn't seen enough of it outside of work. There were other, less tangible reasons too. I felt the time had come to move onwards with certain ambitions, wherever they lay. I'd worked hard, but by now both my head and heart were elsewhere. The time had come to decide what to do.

The opportunity to move on arrived via my friend, Craig, who was preparing to leave Japan and was massively enthused about travelling back to his home city of San Francisco the long way round. I liked the idea; one edge of the Pacific to the other, but via land. He asked me if I was interested in joining him – this plan was only in its formative stages at this point – and it didn't take me long to give him his answer.

A combination of factors accelerated my urge to leave. I mostly put it down to working a steady nine-to-five job which although comfortable enough in the day-to-day sense, never offered me longer term options. I had come to Japan to see the world, and had ended up working throughout the majority of my time there. I like being out of my comfort zone, but was currently stuck in it. I loved Japan and still do: the quirks, the language, and the empowering and vibrant people. But there were many countries I had never visited, and this was a great opportunity. The more I thought about it, the more Craig's idea seemed perfect. The Trans-Siberian was on many people's bucket list, and the more I thought about it, the more radical idea of leaving my day job for the dusty tracks of Siberia won out over the domestic promises offered by this, my humble and very welcoming adoptive nation.

I had seen some of Japan and the Far East but this chance to travel through central and northern Asia, Europe and maybe even on to the Americas appealed to my sense of adventure and fitted my current mood to move on. But after consideration, I felt that I couldn't go all the way to San Francisco on this trip – I would aim to get to all the way back to London if circumstances allowed. Going to San Francisco could wait, for now.

The Trans-Siberian railway, the deep-set sleepers of which make up a fair majority of this journey, is a route many have heard of. For many of those, the majority have sought to travel it; and some have travelled it themselves. The journey these days is perfectly accessible if you do your background research, and as a tourist there are varying levels of class and comfort, and varying destinations and way-points. Craig and I did various legs along it, including the Trans-Mongolian stretch, but also travelled 'backwards' on another line to Vladivostok. Similarly, trips on the railway ending or starting in Ulaanbaatar in Mongolia or Beijing, China as opposed to Moscow are just as easily booked.

I had started the journey with wide eyes and an open mind, but my experiences exceeded way more than these few thousand words would ever do justice. This book aims to give an account of a great journey; the tracks of which often stray from those who trod them before us. It provides snippets of perspectives on friendship (names are real, but surnames omitted for privacy) but overall it seeks to show that in a journey which spans a great distance of the globe, people of varying cultures and persuasions are inherently out to live in contentedness and in order, together. Common humanity, then, is a message which resonates timelessly from east to west.

It was a piercingly bright morning in Kobe when the bus I was travelling on pulled over to the kerb, the driver oblivious to the passengers lurching forward as he braked. My head leant against the window, juddering with the vibrations of the halting vehicle. Some of the other passengers got up and disembarked, whilst I was still rubbing the sleep from my eyes and gathering my things.

I stepped down from the bus onto the tarmac, and the hydraulic door of the bus snapped shut behind me with a hiss. I had left Tokyo the night before on this budget bus service, a cheaper but less comfortable alternative to the train. Hair ruffled from a night's journey with little sleep, and having not eaten in around 16 hours, I let my rucksack hang, then drop to the pavement. Overhead, there wasn't a cloud in the sky. Glancing at my watch, a sense of anticipation came over me. As I checked the time, the second hand of the timepiece caught a glint of the dawn. It was 5.30 am. The screech of tyres echoed from around a corner. The streets of Kobe were deserted.

I looked up at a grey, faceless concrete building, and then looked round at Craig beside me. An American friend of two years, and my fellow traveller, he was fiddling with a buckle on his rucksack. I was glad to have a companion. From marked silence a seagull cried out. The salty sea air was distinct even from where we stood, on a nondescript crumbling road, a couple of kilometres from the port terminal.

With our rucksacks strapped and swollen, we headed

down the gentle slope of the city towards the centre and the docks. A policeman greeted us as we walked by his box – a box just like the old police boxes in the UK. Like all the uniforms in Japan, his jacket was starched stiff and his cap was square, and he was as good-natured as any Japanese police officer you'll ever meet. As he saw the foreigners approach, he smiled and gestured to us.

"How do you do?" he asked politely.

His tone was crisp and formal, but his body language was leisurely and unfussy – the paradox of Japan presented here in a nutshell. He was perky enough, given the time of day.

"Good, thanks," we replied.

"Could you tell us which way to the harbour?"

We talked for a short while; he gave us the directions and our first returned smile of the day.

The pair of us continued to saunter. Amongst the morning hubbub the locals were just setting up shop or getting started for the day, and as we walked around the 'closed' signs of the *kissaten* coffee houses and convenience stores flicked over to read 'open'. The analogy was stark. As a new day dawned in Kobe, so did this new journey in our lives. After getting our bearings we found a coffee shop with a rather large and inviting leather sofa, which served rather large and inviting coffees. Dumping my rucksack down I stretched out on the sofa. We bunkered down in our base for the day; we had enough time to go over the maps and timetables we had with us for the trip ahead.

On the road behind us was Tokyo; the day's dawn had brought Kobe. This city was active, yet somewhere within the frequency of the city din there was a friendly calm about this place; a tranquility akin to the calm sea looming in front of the modern cityscape. This calm, after the hubbub and hypnotic allure of the nation's often emotionally-detached capital, was very welcome.

I had lived in Tokyo for nearly two years before deciding to leave. It had been an immensely satisfying place to create a life, and to work. The stereotypical aspects of Japanese culture were in reality just the bits which complement a greater overall experience; the brush lines which define the masterpiece as a whole. To travel along the impeccably-timed subways, to be immersed in the futuristic neon and shimmering glass of the city restaurants and karaoke bars, to walk slowly amongst the shrines nestled neatly in the narrow city alleys, or to witness first-hand the obtuse wealth of one of the world's largest economies – these were all experiences which had bordered on the sublime. But of course, they were the just the backdrop to my time in Japan.

Every spring Japan is blessed with the coming of the *sakura*; the cherry blossoms. It lasts for around two weeks, usually at the end of each March (although sometimes earlier), and travels the length of the island chain, south to north. Its passing is regarded as one of the most beautiful natural occurrences in the world by Japanese and foreigners alike. Even now, I remember vividly the walk along the Meguro River in west Tokyo, the blossoms of the trees which adorn the river falling from the branches and drifting down onto the wet, cobbled streets below before being flattened under the turning wheels of Tokyo's silent and ever-omnipotent bicycles. The *sakura* are revered by some as being so beautiful that their coming each year signals the opportunity to 'chase' the blossoming flower buds as they make their way north in the emerging, subdued spring. Natives and tourists in unison find the beauty of these flowers so compelling that they must visibly capture the blossoms the length of the country. Watching the trees explode into bloom in Tokyo, it was fascinating to think that only a week or so earlier the same trees were coming into flower in Okinawa and the western Japanese city of Fukuoka. For now, the blooms would eventually swing north towards the wintry, thawing regions of Akita and Aomori and onto the island of Hokkaido, a flat plain of land more reminiscent of Siberia than the Japanese archipelago. The beauty of the *sakura* is in its fleeting nature. The flowers are delicate and pretty, but their coming for only two weeks of the year represents the simultaneous fragility and beauty of life.

A key aspect of the *sakura* season is the hosting of parties and picnics underneath the white and pink hues of the heavily laden bows of the cherry trees. Corporate parties and groups of friends congregate and drink beer, *sake*, and *ume-shu*, – a plum liqueur – on picnic blankets. It is so popular that in the two , prings I spent in Tokyo, it was nigh-on impossible to secure a spot for your party amongst the city parks of Ueno or Shinjuku, to the point that businesses and large groups would reserve and secure spots in the park with the council beforehand. The whole season is a golden opportunity to get together, have fun, and break the ice with work colleagues who revert to their acquaintance-status for the rest of the year.

Other characteristics of the city made it hard to resist. Many travellers to Tokyo may sympathise – I loved the crazy electricity-fueled downtown areas of Shibuya and Shinjuku, bastions of the arcade and MTV culture so prevalent in youthful Japanese culture. Hachiko crossing in Shibuya, for example, was a stronghold of insulated steel and the glass, almost liquid in its shimmering form, which towered above the five-way crossing below. Every two minutes, when the green light was given, the heaving side-walks burst at the seams on to the intersection with hundreds mingling across, anonymous within the murmur, all gliding and weaving without bumping into each other once. Perfection, like a shoal of fish. Ten storeys above this, cinema screens blasted out the latest adverts whilst the giant neon HMV screen on the corner played the latest hip-hop and j-pop videos. The Shibuya station building housed a department store in its upper levels, presiding over the town with an aimless magnetism. Perched on top of this *departo* sat an astro-turf Futsal five-a-side pitch, and a common feature of skyscrapers in Tokyo. It was also indicative of Japan's need for space saving solutions: why not use the tops of buildings, which would be otherwise redundant?

Venture about a mile north of Hachiko, and the incorrigible Harajuku fashionistas strut along leafy Jingu-Mae in their tight jeans, bright jewellery and massive sunglasses. Travel a few blocks still to find the cosplay fanatics filling the escapist ambience of a futuristic Akihabara, almost a caricature of the nerdy Japanese youth. Here the architecture isn't too different from anywhere else in Tokyo, but the abundance of neon signs blinking and shining, hanging from all storeys of the buildings present a crowded image; a city on steroids. The manga and anime stores (cartoons and animations) here are typically visited by the meek and introverted collectors, affectionately termed *otaku*; translated simply and politely as 'geek' in English. Here in Akihabara you can also find the fetish stores and maid cafés (where waitresses dress as French maids whilst they wait on you), and the vending machines which dispense used female underwear in capsules to the perverted and the curious alike.

In Tokyo, these novel phenomena are beautifully complemented by the old town of Asakusa, an area often called *shitamachi* – the 'low town'. You cannot visit this area without noticing Senso-ji, an enormous Buddhist temple which rises out of the city amongst the narrow and wonky old streets of a Tokyo from another era. Touristy rickshaws and cheap kimono stalls vie for space along the boulevard leading to the temple, the upward curve of the temple's pagoda roof an instantly recognisable symbol of the orient. Paper lanterns coloured deep red and gold adorn wooden beams, as photographers, tourists, and Tokyo natives all pay their respects here. This city, whilst being a visual feast, was less kind to the nostrils. Hachiko square for example would absolutely stink after a heavy rainfall, due to the sewers being well above the city's subway network, only six feet below us.

The city gardens of Shinjuku-gyoen and Yoyogi will always remind me of short but stiflingly humid summers sipping on a beer, throwing a frisbee or, in the case of Yoyogi Park, observing the gifted drummers busking and toiling away on a long Sunday afternoon. The city is a place where space is remarkably limited (albeit efficiently organised), and gardens are a rarity. As a result, it seemed people came to these well-designed and welcoming public parks much more frequently than in their western counterpart city's parks. Yoyogi is a well-designed park rich in open grassy areas with fountains at the centre and wooded sections to the sides, ideal for dog-walking, jogging, and socialising. I would often run to Yoyogi from my place in Ikejiri-ohashi, do a lap around the edge, and return through Shibuya – an undulating route in which you see a wide variety of the city. Originally the land belonging to an Edo era feudal lord, and then used as agricultural land, the Imperial gardens of Shinjuku-gyoen were rebuilt into its modern layout after being bombed in World War Two. In contrast it is a much more manicured garden than Yoyogi; a place where the aesthetics are to be absorbed through your eyes and delicate fragrances through your nose, rather than the feel of the grass blades underneath your feet. I recall it was, on a bright spring day, a most beautiful thing to witness its panorama of peculiar urban juxtaposition. Whether you are admiring the English-style section, or the traditional Japanese gardens, you will nearly always be able to see the skyscrapers and office blocks of Shinjuku in the background.

In the case of Craig and I, 'beer-walking' was what we had sometimes utilised Yoyogi park for. We lived opposite sides of the city, and both loved walking, so when we met every few weeks, we would catch up, discuss and walk around the park and the surrounding downtown streets, beer in hand. It was a pleasure I enjoyed; being rarely content to sit still at the best of times, and this way it was social, it was exercise, it was discussion; and it was unconventional. I think it may have been meditation too, if I were to dwell on this a little deeper. It was also entirely possible due to the law in Japan stipulating opened containers of alcohol could be consumed in plain sight on city streets, with no penalty.

Craig and I liked 'beer-walking' so much, on one occasion we endeavoured to trek resolutely around the loop of the 40 kilometre Yamanote railway line in one day. The Yamanote line snakes and swerves its way around and through central Tokyo in an ellipse, from an egg-shaped point in Shinagawa in the south to the northern suburbs of Nippori and Sugamo. It is basically Tokyo's circle line, but above ground, either at ground level or sometimes on stilts. It was summer at the time, and it was excruciatingly humid, so to escape the heat (as if we weren't gluttons for punishment enough) we departed at around five in the evening, aiming to be finished in the small hours of the morning. I recommend this rather strange walk to anyone – it is long, and it is arduous, yet from street level upwards it gives a satisfyingly intimate portrait of the districts of Tokyo, from the well visited to the hardly bothered-with-at-all. I have done it twice now: both clockwise and anti-clockwise, by day and by night. On this occasion we started our metropolitan hike from the hubbub of the Starbucks coffee at the foot of Shibuya crossing in central Tokyo, meandering south through the clean streets of Ebisu and Meguro. The trendy haze of Shibuya gave way to the slightly more upmarket and bohemian Ebisu, as *departo* – department stores that catered for the masses – turned into the unique boutiques Tokyo is renowned for. The modernity and hygienic front of this city are complemented by the litter and traffic fumes of every other major conurbation in the world, and as it grew dark the city became slightly more characterless than usual.

As we sauntered the day became dusk, normally a pleasant time in Tokyo as the orange haze of the sky meets the subdued streetlights. Every two minutes, like clockwork, the green logo of a Yamanote line train swished by. As we walked, we saw the districts of Tokyo and its suburbs rise and fall, the streets of the city giving way to our path, all merging into one. The southerly tip of the Yamanote line lay in Shinagawa, a fairly bland and conservative business district where insipid and instantly forgettable buildings line streets filled with the dark suits and coats of Japanese *salarymen*. We stopped to eat at an Indian; the restaurant was ideally placed between the railway line we were following and the street running parallel to it. It was the ideal fuel as we turned the southern-most corner of the line and proceeded almost due north towards the giddy metropolitan lights of Shinbashi, Tokyo, and Yurakucho. These areas are the downtown financial and business areas of the city but being so central they still house karaoke bars and restaurants, and are busy even in the late evening.

As we walked through Shinbashi, under one of the Yamanote railway line arches lay 'The Bud Bar', a place where the tables are the cheap plastic beach type and the music is suitably cheesy. The gimmick is that busty women serve you large jugs of ice cold Budweiser. This night was no exception and the sounds of a busy bar could be heard as we passed on by.

The vibrant air of Tokyo remains long into the night, and it is truly a city that never sleeps. To the east is the Imperial Palace, a Mecca for city joggers and tourists, and Hibiya Koen, a wonderfully western-influenced park which sports fountains and European gardens alongside a smaller area of tranquil Japanese gardens and rock pools. During the summer, the park also plays host to a German beer event with beer tasting and sausages on the menu. I have fond memories of the park and know it well, as on many occasions I used to eat my lunch there and walk around it in the middle of the day, it being only a block from my office.

Passing further north, our route alongside the Yamanote tracks took us past Ueno Park, and Japan's most famous zoo of the same name. I hadn't spent much time there in the past, just a couple of *sakura* celebrations, and now was unfortunately no exception – we had some miles yet to walk. From Ueno all that remained was to traverse the northern suburbs, the commuter belt, if you like, before we swung south into Ikebukuro and its towering city lights. The suburbs here were gentle, and being around 3.00 am, were comfortably quiet. The main difference was that we were able to walk through deserted residential alleys which didn't always run parallel to the tracks. The walk was also noticeably hillier in nature. However Ikebukuro was thankfully still alive and we strode back into the city confident of making our goal before dawn, although by now, the miles had taken their toll. It was the small hours of the morning, and we ached as our lead-like legs trudged past Ikebukuro station's north exit. This northern part of the city loomed high like a real-life Gotham, modern and faceless like much of Tokyo but still with cosmopolitan clout. For now, though, the end was in sight. Craig and I passed through Shinjuku's more questionable areas and continued through the back streets and into funky Harajuku without incident. Testament to the safety and low crime rate of Japan, not once did Craig or I feel uncomfortable. Strolling through a hushed, subdued Yoyogi Park, we finally limped back to Shibuya Starbucks around 4.00 am. Only then did I realise that due to train timings, I was going to have to walk home to Ikejiriohashi, another two or so miles! Our goodbyes were brief, for now there was only one thing on both our minds. Sleep.

***

Summer is firework season in Japan; although I prefer the Japanese word *hanabi* – 'fire-flower' to the English 'firework'. I remember a *hanabi* celebration spent the previous summer in the company of a friend named Yayoi, she in her rich peach-coloured *yukata* us we both sat by the Sumida River during the firework display. The kimono, despite generally being a quite shapeless garment, hugged her figure. Her hair was tied up tight to her head in the traditional style, leaving the back of her pale neck deliciously exposed. Sipping on chilled, earthy green tea and relaxing in the rare shimmering cool of a Japanese summer evening underneath the bows of a sturdy tree, nothing could have removed me from that moment. The *hanabi* exploded into life over the city skyline, the Sumida River in the foreground. The lights of the fireworks illuminated the buildings of Tokyo, which shimmered in the grey haze that settled on the city after dusk. The river reflected the display in its swell and the trees in my immediate vision were vast and imposing in the *hanabi* pastel hue for just a second before the light died. Never had I seen more charming a sight than a young collection of Japanese girls, all decorated in yukatas of varying colour and style, gazing at the evening sky with their eyes as wide and as inviting as a freshwater lake on a summer's day. They were accompanied by stylishly dressed young city boyfriends, as they all nibbled at picnics and sipped on Asahi beer and *sake*, the girls giggling about nothing whilst the fireflowers blazed into the clear August dusk.

I lived in Sangenjaya, near Ikejiri-Ohashi, in a cool part of western Tokyo, in a shared house. All the tenants had separate bedrooms but shared the living room and kitchen and communal roof garden. The guesthouse – Sun Heights – was always full of characters, from those who drifted in between jobs, to tourists, to people who actually chose to live there full time, like me. One time there was a guy who moved in for about two weeks who had lost his job and had to temporarily downsize; another we had an ex-Israeli special forces soldier who was in town for a vacation. His English was better than my Hebrew, and most evenings after work we would work out or go running through Sangenjaya. Other friends gave vibrancy to my time here: Masa worked in dull IT by day but lived for the weekend; Sara was an out-of-work actress; and Kimi was a fairly successful drug dealer. The landlords of this bohemian mishmash were Frenchmen in Japan for the martial artists scene, who took the rent in cash – and asked no questions.

A confirmed Tokyo resident, I loved the the ebb and flow and rising tide of one of the world's most intriguing cities. It could be said that to both look at and experience, Tokyo is like any other western city – multiplied to the power of ten. The day-to-day course of a 20-something expat was ingrained in my skin. I frequented the opulent Ginza shopping district, spent time in the company of Tokyo's more distinctive areas, such as the wide boulevards and select eateries of Omote-Sando and Aoyama, and spent many an evening screaming into a karaoke microphone, murdering the notes. Tree-lined Omote-Sando could easily be a street straight out of London or Los Angeles, with modern, stylised concrete and steel architecture garnishing the wide boulevard, decorated with designer and independent boutiques. My corporation had an office here; and I had strolled here many times. The flashy, almost diamond encrusted, cavernous flagship stores of Louis Vuitton, Givenchy, and Tag Heuer wrestled for space with other imports – further down lay GAP and Gold's Gym.

I had a favourite bar, which was a grungy little haunt called 'Garageland' in a similarly grungy little back alley in Shibuya. The bar's street sign was made as a mock-up of the Sex Pistols 'God Save the Queen' cover, with its bright yellow and pink neon light flickering, almost coaxing you inside. It was dark, and small, but rich in character. A narrow place which was thin on furniture, yet also somehow stifling, the recesses of the bar's dark walls contained forgotten rock memorabilia and surplus stock. The signature piece of this bar was its longest main wall. It had the scribbling and signatures of all the famous bands who had spent an evening there; I recognised many from Britpop and indie bands of the UK, although I knew fewer from the Japanese scene. The one that sticks in my mind the most was the UK band Razorlight's signature, scribbled on the wall in black marker pen and, like most, the penmanship indicating a lack of sobriety at the time. Some others were simple signatures, some messages, and the odd little limerick thrown in for good measure. But I remember going in the bar the night after Razorlight had been in, to my dismay I had missed them by chance, by only 24 hours.

The owner, Tom (a nickname, short for Tsutomo) explained that the bar was unofficially known by bands or artists touring or going through Tokyo, a place off the beaten track where the drinkers (and we were 'drinkers' – not 'clientele') could choose the music and say whatever the hell they wanted. The bar was welcoming but still fiercely raw; at times I could feel utterly isolated, others in the most social mood possible.

I would go there regularly, a few times a month or a couple of times a week, drinking the cold draft beer in the dim red light and practising my Japanese on other young music lovers who frequented the bar. I would meet new people, and hang out. Tom was never seen without a cigarette drooping from his lips (Japan actually has a higher smoking consumption than France), and appeared always at once to be both alive and dead. His jet-black hair flopped onto a stressed forehead. Always nursing a borderline dangerous lack of sleep; the numerous cigarettes and drinks he consumed kept him propped up faintly against the beer taps, poised and ready to answer any music-related question thrown his way in the midst of the evening. He explained in Japanese and in dashes of English that he had a job during the day with a corporation and managed this place each night after that. He managed to catch up on sleep usually on a Sunday. Always sporting a low, shaggy mop of hair and always dressed in a compulsory black baggy t-shirt and jeans, it was impossible to tell if he'd changed his clothes since the last time you saw him. He also served the best fish and chips I ever tasted in Tokyo. It wasn't traditional at all, more like a fried fish cake with French fries, but it was flavourful and it was the closest I came without going to a gimmicky tourist 'Ye Olde English' style English pub (of which there are plenty about).

To commute, I had bought a folding bicycle from a friend who was emigrating from another room in my guesthouse to Thailand to take up a job there. I offered her Y3,000 (about £15 at the time) for the thing last minute, and she accepted. It happened to be bright green and not massively well looked after, but a lick of paint and some oil sorted that to some extent. I would primarily use the badly-painted folding bike to go to work in Omote-Sando from my place in Ikejiri-Ohashi, cycling through the famous Shibuya crossing early in the morning and late in the evening – absolute bliss when there was no traffic around. Due to excellent cycle routes and the uncongested sidings which lined the Meguro *gawa* from my neighbourhood through to Shimo-Kitazawa, or Sangenjaya, for example, I could also go out of an evening with friends from my guesthouse and not worry about cycling back through traffic when tipsy.

Another of my favourite haunts was affectionately known as 'The Rat Bar' due to the non-human clientele who also happened to frequent it and its surrounding alleys. The bar was a small room off an alleyway in Shimo-Kitazawa, the route to which could be found by burrowing your way through the sheltered and monotonous alleys, which even after a few visits still had to be remembered by rote. I would follow the Meguro *gawa* broadly west from Sun Heights, winding across a couple of arterial routes before turning north on the main drag to Shimo-Kitazawa, a bustling street full of fashionable shops and small eateries. From there the memories are hazy; but before the station you turn right off the main street into a network of back alleys, where a few rusty old bars sit underneath the rail arches. The Rat Bar had a front room – possibly the owners' own front room – with a shelf of a bar, and a few wooden tables outside in the alleyway. Next door, but almost within the same bar, was a karaoke place: a few karaoke DVDs in a player plugged into an old cathode-ray tube television, cheap alcohol, and not much more. I loved it for a variety of reasons, mostly the alcohol price, but the mixture of friendly faces combined with gruff old-timer Tokyo-ites gave it a special feel too. I could have a great night out, great conversation, and could pedal home within 15 minutes, grab some Gyoza dumplings on the way home – and all for less than the price of a decent meal in a pub. On the other side of the railway tracks was another cheap choice; a shisha bar where we all sat on the *tatami* mat floor, or on a wooden stool if there was one. A shisha pipe and flavoured tobacco would cost around Y500, and an espresso coffee was around Y100 (peanuts at around £1.50 or 50p respectively). Sunset times are largely similar through the year in Tokyo, meaning cycling to Shimokitazawa was often dark and sweaty in the humidity, which only added to the grungy nature of our nights out.

Cycling on my trusty steed took me all over the neighbourhood. The Meguro *gawa*, if you continue upstream, flows near enough past the front door of Sun Heights, then becomes a kind of sculpted canal as it you wind narrower and shallower further west towards its mouth. The river finally disappears underground altogether at the point I would then turn right, or north, to Shimokitazawa – although the *gawa* and I would always part ways on good terms.

That folding bike and I had some great times. I pedaled it dressed in a suit to important meetings and long days at work; in scruffy clothes as I killed time in my neighbourhood on days off; and with a towel and flip-flops as I made my way to the local hot baths. As my awful paint job wore off, leaving flakes of black all over Tokyo, the original lime green started to show through on scuffs and joints. This terrible, lime green-coloured piece of trash with awful gearing and rusty parts left me with a passion for folding bikes which has lasted until this very day. It went all over the greater Tokyo area whilst in my possession and really affected my experience of the city as it allowed me to see all the streets above ground, which the subway would not offer me. I have always been a strong believer that when abroad wandering above ground is way more satisfying than using public transport as you learn more and are not merely going to one destination. Despite my affection for this rubbish, folding bike though, one night I left the thing chained to a lamp post in Shibuya while I went out drinking and caught the subway home. When I went back the next day, the thing had been removed and impounded by the

Tokyo police. Apparently around that time of year, the Tokyo PD has low level crime targets to meet, so recorded incidents of speeding and parking tickets go up in order for them to meet these bureaucratic deadlines.

Never has the word 'tragedy' been more apt. I never even got to say goodbye.

***

Craig and I were meeting at Tokyo central station for our overnight bus to Kobe; the bus that would take me away from my adopted city, and everything I had known for the last two years. The emotions were a mixed bag. What was I doing? Did I have enough money to complete the trip? Had I packed the right kit? What would I do back in England if and when I made it back? Would I ever come back to Tokyo? Would I ever see my Japanese friends again? Who knew? I certainly didn't. And yet, as Craig said goodbye to Rie, his girlfriend (and future wife) and I stood politely over away a little as they did so, there was a positivity in the atmosphere. Craig was upbeat, albeit vague – if it was meant to be, they'd see each other again. Spoiler alert: it was.

I was excited. The travel bug had bit before, but this was likely to be the longest trip I had made to date, and to places I had yearned to see.

PART TWO

Back in Kobe, I had casually checked in to a capsule hotel. As the name suggests, economy (in both financial and spatial terms) is the name of the game. It was my last night in Japan, but my first night experiencing one of these hotels. They are a stress-reliever and a safety net for the workers of Japan who plod on into the night, marching to the tune of their corporation, fearlessly risking missing the last train. Built mainly for these overworked commuters, they are also a thrifty option for the cash strapped traveller. I paid Y3,000 (around £12 at the time) to stay a night, and despite the obvious space deficiencies, they are remarkably rewarding to occupy. Once the weary traveller or overworked *salaryman* has checked in, the shoes come off and you make your way around the hotel in the complementary plastic slippers which are commonplace throughout Japanese hospitality. The rooms are about 3 feet by 3 feet by 6 feet long, with a polyester curtain door, the TV remote and other controls inside folding away to leave enough room to sleep, stretch, or sit up. This particular capsule however, whilst being a pleasure to inhabit, happened to be quite a startling shade of bright orange – not the colour I'd use to invite people to get some sleep.

The most likeable factor of any Japanese accommodation is, to me, the public baths, in which you bath in an evening after a hard day's toil. Nearly all hotels or *ryokans* (local inns) have a public bath section or, if you're extremely lucky, the public bath will be from real mountain spring water; an *onsen*. I had bathed in many during my time here; after a hard day after work, or after navigating the ski slopes of the Japanese Alps, nothing refreshed me more than sitting in an open air *onsen* in famously hot, clean water whilst the snow descended gracefully into the budding cherry trees of early spring. There is a changing area where you enter and get undressed, before you proceed, fully unclothed, through the entrance to the main baths. The first thing a foreigner will come across is a stool, sat in front of a bucket, basin, and mirror. Most nowadays will have soap and detergents on the side, and crisp gleaming floors. Some of the more dated places may not possess such luxury. This is where you sit or squat, and thoroughly clean, scrub and shampoo yourself – only then proceeding to enter the communal pool of inviting warm water. I would then spend an hour or more, if time allowed, soaking, sweating, becoming cleansed; slowly watching the ends of my fingers transform into wrinkly prunes.

The *onsen* is also a surprisingly social place; given the fact your most intimate areas are visible, just beneath the waters' surface. Indeed, the Japanese have a saying about the merits of such '*hadaka no tsukiai*' (naked communication) for getting to know people better in the relaxed *onsen* atmosphere. As well as being extremely civilised, comfortable, and revitalising, after such soaking they tended also to give me the deepest sleep of my life.

A city of leisurely pace, Kobe plays its part in the very Japanese paradox of mixing the old and the new, tradition and modernity. The neon, for example, so prevalent in Japanese cities, sits alongside aged, wooden buildings and shrines founded in yesteryear – many now destroyed by a history of war and natural disaster. Contemporary architecture and the sheen of the modern port facility in Kobe's foreground give way to deep-set images like the ageless Ikuta Shrine and the climbing, green Rokko Mountain range in the background. Being wedged between the mountains and the sea, Kobe is a long and thin city, hugging the coast. Its geography only serves to enhance its beauty; and the grand Port Tower presides over a city famed for its cosmopolitan air, with affluent shopping and entertainment districts complementing the majestic Akashi-Kaikyo bridge. This structure, synonymous with Kobe, stretches gracefully out from the city southwards to Awaji Island over the rich and murky blues of the Akashi strait.

That day, I strode pensively around the central districts of Sannomiya and Motomachi, camera in hand. The delicate red-brick archways underneath the main railway line house shops, cafes, and standing bars. The commotion of the city laid bare in all its glory by the summer sun was pleasing. The gently dozing city of the early morning had fully awoken, with all its inhabitants skilfully weaving and bobbing along the streets, as if on a pre-ordained course. Items were bought; people were eating *takoyaki* (octopus fried in dough), openly arguing in their Kansai dialect; elderly people watched the world go by on benches in the street. This tender vision of a sophisticated ancient port city, touched by the outside world of trade and adventure in a famously introverted society, is not however entirely whole. The contemporary and offbeat Japan simultaneously ridiculed and embraced by western audiences is still a unique and fascinating place, and despite the country's large expanse of idyllic rural towns and untouched mountains, there is even in these places an infiltrated presence of a society ahead of its time. Take for example a quite modern incarnation, the *conbini*; a Japanese nick-name for the common convenience store. A representation of post-war American influence, it is a lifeline to many singletons and city dwellers alike, offering everything from photocopying to hot meals. *Conbini* are everywhere. They are a safety net in an age of convenience and modernity; and a reminder that with the economic prosperity of the late 20th century brought a new style of consumerism. However bad things got, you'd never be hungry or deprived of warmth in Japan, as long as you were within walking distance of these bastions, these ever-dependable chain stores. In the major cities there's at least one per block.

Tucked up tight in my orange chrysalis of a hotel room, a zany Japanese game show meandered through its formulaic motions in the background whilst I reflected. I pondered my impending journey and leaving my adopted home. Craig had come to Japan three years previously with the intent of travelling back to his native San Francisco the long way round. Pacific coast to Pacific coast, using the land. I had been co-collaborator of this plan for the last six months, intending my destination to be the UK, where I grew up.

Both of us intended to traverse the plateaus of Mongolia and Siberia and the oriental cities of China and Central Asia on our way back to the wintry Europe and North America we had known. The USA was on the verge of massive political change with the ascension of Barack Obama to the presidency; Europe was becoming a different map too, with the post-Soviet and Eastern European countries now becoming equal within the EU. It would be exciting to return, and the prospect of our journey filled us with fervour. We had no real route intended, no plan of attack, something which meant we could maximise our experience on the road. Nevertheless, I would miss Japan, an island of contradictions;

of insanity and logic, once famed for its warrior samurai, yet in today's modern era depressingly famed more for its efficient business acumen.

"Well, we're taking the slow boat to China now, man", Craig had mused earlier that day, as we sat talking near the Kobe docks. We were – absolutely – about to take a boat to China, but I didn't quite understand him.

"Sorry?" I said. I'd never heard the expression before.

"The slow boat to China, man. You never heard of that saying?"

He was right. I hadn't.

"Nope... Sorry."

"Oh, we'll it's what we're doing, in a roundabout kind of way. It means taking a journey, a slow journey."

Again, he had a point. What could be slower than taking a boat to China?

"Anyway, it's a journey where you could be doing it faster, or easier; but you're not. You're actively choosing to travel aimlessly along. And the journey is way more enjoyable because it's not done in a rush."

"OK", I said.

I agreed. We were absolutely taking the slow boat to China. And it felt good.

Stood on the deck of the passenger ferry that would take me into the ferry port of Tianjin, China, I watched the islands of western and southern Japan float on by beside the ship on waters of crystal blue and calm, slowly fading into the distance. The boat wasn't travelling fast, but the winds were blustery enough. The sun shone brightly, cascading rays onto the water and the ripples which spread from the ship. It was amazing weather for the season. The bold red Chinese flag at the stern flapped in the cool summer air; the uncomfortable edge of the humid Japanese summer taken off by both the speed we were travelling and the gentle sea breeze.

More islands appeared on the horizon, with their curves, edges, and serene slopes. Passengers milled around on the steel deck, painted a dull shade of white. People exchanged small pleasantries and got a feel for the ship. Some of them were Japanese travellers, others Chinese merchants homeward bound. Frugally-minded westerners like I had found an economical way of going to China that was more romantic and reminiscent of bygone times than a cheap and simple airfare to Beijing. The other westerners on the boat were mostly heading for China for the Beijing Olympics of 2008. For example, the 20-something Australian teacher with short blonde ringlets en route to meet her family to celebrate the games; the mass of American and Japanese students grasping this opportunity for a brief exchange to the city (cameras and wide-eyed smiles a prerequisite for such a trip); or the vivacious

French couple who were making a vacation of the games from Japan – staying in the first class cabin, indeed.

Our cabin however was a communal room, with ten futon mattresses in one open unfurnished room. Screaming neglect on the far wall were two grimy portholes. Craig and I were objects of fascination for our roommates; why on earth would seemingly affluent westerners be taking this slow boat to China on an ill-used shipping line?

Two Japanese guys at the far end of our space were sympathising with our journey as they were travelling in a similarly ambitious nature. The first, who couldn't have been more than around 23 or 24, had previously spent time in Afghanistan whilst the coalition forces fought terrorism around 2005. With shoulder length messy black hair and a gnarled, neglected goatee beard, he mixed periods of complete sombre silence with gushes of passionate narrative about his travels. He particularly advocated to us the benefits of having Asiatic facial features in a land such as Afghanistan, where those from the west are often regarded with disdain. It made sense to me. He also had no plans regarding travelling, and was initially winding his way to China, from there possibly on to the beaches and lagoons of Thailand. Later in the journey, in a shy gesture he would pass on to me a book, to commemorate the Beijing Olympic Games of 2008, into which I would write a short entry, leaving my contact details before passing it onto other travellers I came across. It was an artistic project, really, using our entries and travels to create a work of art which was both physical and symbolic. The aim was that the last person in possession of this book before the London 2012 Olympic Games would email the contributors in an effort for us all to reunite in the city of London, in a representation of

Humankind's undying nomadic nature as well as marking these two immense international sporting events. Remarkably I did receive an email about a reunion in 2012 from the final recipient of the book – the irony was at that time it was I who was the one in Afghanistan, and therefore could not attend.

This Afghan wanderer's kindred spirit, who was in the futon adjacent to me, was an older Japanese gentleman. He was possibly in his late 40s, short in stature with cropped hair greying at the temples, crew cut fashion. He had the poise of a man intelligent and aware of the world; he was a man of experience. He sat cross-legged, didn't move much, and seemed unmoved by what was going on around him. Busy or slow, light or dark, he seemed to observe and simply soak up the goings-on around him. Again, in Japanese, with dashes of English here and there, we learnt of his trip. He spoke only when he wanted to contribute and used his words succinctly. This was the second time he'd used this ship to go from Kobe to Beijing, as he was circumnavigating the globe and was currently on his second, glorious lap. He had set out around eight months previously to circle the world, and had in his own idiot-savant wording, 'just kept going'. I secretly admired him. He had seen the Indian sub-continent; had spent time in East Africa; killed time in Paris in the spring, making it to South America before crossing the Pacific to his homeland of Japan. Yet once home, he weighed up his options and proceeded to just... keep going.

The sun lowered in the sky, and I reflected on the last sunset I would watch in Japan. As I moved west, I realised I would see more and more sunsets, each one getting closer to home. But if I wanted, I could just keep going west – continue with Craig, if I wished – and it was a tempting thought. I left it to linger at the back of my mind.

I thought back to a few hours earlier when I was going through customs. I had (rather to Craig's amusement) been singled out for the random baggage search. The customs official looked young, new to his uniform, and slightly on edge. He was quite polite, although he actually seemed a bit annoyed to have to inspect someone with such cumbersome baggage. It wasn't the size of my pack *per se*, which was really rather small, but the fact I had to get everything out of such small compartments. It was at this time that I suddenly remembered a parting gift from a dear friend and student, Yukiko. She had given me, three days previously, a package of expensive soap, carefully and delicately wrapped in tissue paper. Of course, soap is not illegal. It did however look quite like a block of hashish. The official's hands hovered over the side compartment containing my fragrant contraband. With a pause, he asked me to open it up and display the contents. Then, with a slab of brown, resinous substance in hand, he asked me what this item was, with the upward intonation of a genuinely puzzled man. Luckily, he saw the funny side and let me pass, satisfied I was not a trafficker of any kind. The whole episode had been watched by Craig – who had passed unscathed – who was sporting a nervous smile, unsure of whether to make fun or be genuinely worried for me. In the end he opted for the former: satisfying, since I would have done the same to him.

Back on deck, our ship cruised further forward, away from Kobe, and my life in Japan. Beyond the bows lay the Western Isles, Korea, and China beyond. We glided underneath the Seto-Chuo expressway bridge, rising out of the rocky coast of

Shikoku and connecting to the largest island of the archipelago, Honshu. Later under cover of darkness we would again almost silently pass underneath the similar Kammonkyo Bridge which links northern Kyushu with Honshu. I marveled at the remarkable solid architecture, and was reminded of the Akashi-Kaikyo Bridge we had passed in Kobe earlier that day.

The islands glided by. The life of a fisherman among these Western Islands must be beauty coupled with upmost simplicity, unburdened by the materialistic hedonism of the nation's capital to the east. Perhaps I romanticise; this is after all a country which embraces the newest technology in all its modern glory and wonder. But, in my mind's eye, I would like to think there is still a very clear rural and urban divide in Japan, that there still exist little fishing villages born of days gone by where rural fishers and divers still go about their craft in traditional ways, living off of the fresh sashimi of the day's catch on the beach. It's this kind of rural idyll I hadn't seen enough of in my stay here, and a real reason to return to Japan in the future.

The home strait of our voyage into China seemed to take an eternity. From the bows, we could see China miles before we landed on its shores; an endless body of polluted, murky water mirrored by an endless sea of cranes, warehouses and smog above the water line. If Japan was the refined, cultured, urban socialite of Asia, China seemed to be the black sheep of the family; dirty and brutish. As we tallied up to the dock, the porter struggled to tie our gangplank to its support. He succeeded; and we strode onto terra firma for the first time in three days. Cranes, warehouse buildings, and containers stretched as far as the eye could see. Despite being a port, there was no breeze in Tianjin that day.

Tianjin is an industrial, ordinary place, not surprisingly. In that respect it reminded me of a town I spent my teenage years in – a grubby little satellite town near Oxford. The first thing you notice in China is the mass of bicycles. Or, more specifically, the lack of traffic discipline. All transport, engine powered or not, weaved its paths in and out of lanes fluidly and indifferently. It could have been the busiest of traffic in the UK, on the worst of days, if not for the one distinction that in the UK we have a highway code to invoke; in China I imagine traffic infringements are less formally dealt with. On the bus through Tianjin, I witnessed two traffic accidents that trip alone. In Japan I had rarely witnessed a traffic accident; once or twice perhaps, but on reflection I realised it wasn't often enough to have made the slightest imprint on my memory.

There was chaos at the terminal. Neither of us could make heads nor tails of the public transport and how to get to Beijing. Luckily, as so often happens, a generous stranger noticed us ambling about and translated our options to us. She was more than helpful, willing to practise her English, and led us to the correct bus. In no time, we were squashed into another bus, merging onto the freeway to Beijing.

Beijing is a city of over 17 million, all sprawled out within an area the size of Belgium. It is nearly impossible to describe to those that haven't been the sheer scale of the city. Roads are frequently three or four lanes in each direction; and it'll take you 20 minutes to walk around a city block in August. The city seemed alive with Olympic fever; posters and images of the five rings permeated our eyes and our minds. The Chinese had really excelled themselves for the Olympics. Television screens displaying the games were installed in subway carriages, and interpreters could be found on every street corner to help foreign tourists with their stay. Yet this was not all foreign – Gap and Wal-Mart stores can easily be found here, a reserve of the middle class perhaps, but available nonetheless. China seemed uninhibited, not modest or reserved; holding its head high. Clearly, a nation confidently navigating the stormy waters of international criticism and a changing economic era.

Getting around is easy. Taxis are the first option, cheap and accessible, but for the most part I used the subway. Inferior in no way to the punctual system in Tokyo, however it was superior in one way: the price. In Japan, the rail fares worked on a sliding scale per kilometre, with fare-adjustment machines at each station in case you under calculated or changed route. Here, two Yuan (20p) got you a single fare to anywhere in the city, and you charged your electronic pass up with as many fares as you liked.

The *hutong* of Beijing are one of the city's defining

characteristics. Single storey narrow alleyways which house families in communal blocks, they network into each other and criss-cross Beijing like a never-ending labyrinth. As far as I could ascertain, the majority had the Chinese Red and Gold flag proudly displayed upon their walls. The bricks which comprise the *hutong* were visibly weathered, crumbling into the dirt of the alley. Residents of the *hutong* share the communal bathrooms and camaraderie, but little else abounds. The houses within are owned by peasants and for the most part are barely furnished.

I strolled through a *hutong* one morning. My hotel was on the edges of one, and increasingly hard to find if you didn't have a map. As we got nearer the hotel, the further away we imagined we were. However, the *hutong* was startling. Glimpses sneaked through wooden, aged doorways and barred, chipped glass windows revealed residences more than lacking.

Approaching a wooden door which had partially come off its hinges, I peered inside. A dirty Asiatic face peered back out of the gloom. A soiled mattress on the similarly grimy floor, a blanket on top perhaps, and a rickety broken chair were all that were inside. There were no light bulbs, only oil-powered lamps. The people appeared only to own the clothes they were stood up in; and in the August humidity this meant vests, shorts and flip-flops for the males, and not much more for the females.

Although rustic in their simplicity, and a defining architectural characteristic of the city, Beijing's authorities have scheduled all but the most beautiful for demolition. Everywhere Craig and I would see the Chinese character for 'condemned' splashed in red paint across the semi-derelict walls of the hutong. Their logic was sound; apartment blocks could house ten times the number of people than the *hutong* could. Yet there was much uproar among the residents of Beijing, for unlike the Temple of Heaven, or The Forbidden City, the *hutong* were icons of grassroots living. Some have their own tales to tell, or links to the past. Historic, cultural; ingrained in the city's atmosphere even – these were not simply structures: they symbolised the only lifestyle the majority have ever known.

Around the corner, on the outskirts of the *hutong* I was living in, were a group of young guys who seemed to know the odd word in English and would attempt to chat to us as they conducted their business. They were dressed in shabby shorts, t-shirts which hung baggy around their thin bodies, and flip-flops on dust covered feet. Most of the time I carried on with a polite smile, but sometimes I would stop and attempt to get a closer look at their business. It seems that poverty and lacklustre surroundings are only barriers to those without real enterprising thoughts and plenty of grit. These lads were busy cooking chicken strips which lay on a rusty strip of metal, using a hair dryer. Said hair dryer had no plastic casing and simply the metal working parts: the boys had to hold it with a tea towel to avoid burning their hands. The chicken cooked slowly under such conditions, turning only mildly brown, like the rust surrounding it. The meat itself looked only slightly more hygienic than this rust on which it sat. Beside their little hair dryer 'oven' was a piece of cardboard advertising the price of the chicken. The eager boys turned the meat over every few minutes. I didn't try it; for that matter I didn't see anybody else eating it, but I'm sure the guys had their customers.

A couple of blocks away from the *hutong* I was staying in, there was a reasonably priced Chinese restaurant which Craig and I went to three or four times. It was simple but served decent sized, spicy Chinese dishes and cheap beer. It was a plastic tabled, paper mat type of place but all the locals went there, and it was tasty. Once inside there were around 20 tables made of red plastic, and crummy pictures of dragons and the Chinese calendar hung on the walls. Most of the time I had the shredded beef or a spicy chicken dish – but the one time Craig and I opted for the 'beef soup' we weren't convinced it was exactly beef on the menu; a local stray perhaps? The waitress was short, with long light brown hair, glasses, and always sported a smile. She, like all the staff, wore black clothes with a white apron. She tried to talk to us on several occasions and seemed pleasant enough. After eating there one time, she tried to overcharge us by about 20% of the total bill, and after giving the place another chance about a week later we found that she tried it again. That was the last time we went there. "Fool me once", they say.

***

Any visitor to the Forbidden City, at the very heart of Beijing's sprawling mass, will not leave disappointed. Its familiar terracotta walls have stood firm for over five centuries, giving the place a fortified atmosphere. However, the rushing alleyways and labyrinth of rooms gives a softer, intricate ambience. The complex was the dwelling place of the Emperors of the Ming and Qing dynasty, and stood as the house of the government and the political centre too. Its size is quite remarkable, comprising of over 720,000 square metres.

Shrubs and painted mural walls make the whole experience a charming one, whilst the most accessible northerly compound, the Imperial Garden, is a simply stunning example of horticultural ability and oriental design. I spent a good few hours pottering around the complex, discovering little cubby-hole rooms, taking pictures of the burnt red terracotta partitions under an unforgiving bright blue sky. The walls apparently took 15 years to build, utilising the skills of one million workers to create it. As I peered into yet another courtyard, I saw a vine climbing up the wall, pegged into the dusty orange cement. Below it sat several pot plants ornately arranged along the wall. A Chinese woman sat reading on a bench, from the look on her face she must have been involved in a gripping storyline.

From the confines of the Forbidden City, you could hear none of the noise of the traffic or people from Tiananmen Square. Designated a World Heritage site in 1987, it is also the largest collection of wooden structures in the world. It is so well preserved, that if you were to remove the hundreds of modern day tourists ambling and photographing their way through the audio tour, you could genuinely imagine a young Qing dynasty Emperor in full silk dress being escorted down the crisp, silent corridors on official state business, surrounded by his subjects.

Our time in Beijing was not entirely unmarred – we did have another experience which did leave a sour taste during our stay in China. Although it could have been avoided had we not come during the Olympic season. On our way to view the Jinshanling area of the Great Wall, one of the steepest and most impressive sections, we had to use the bus to a certain place, changing there for an onward bus to the region we were headed to. However, this was China, and it was easier said than done.

The bus ride wasn't pleasant, but we got to see parts of Beijing we wouldn't otherwise have seen.

Once at the bus station where we were supposedly changing, a circling crowd of taxi drivers descended like vultures onto our position. Pidgin English and aggressive body language were the bartering tools of the day.

"Taxi, Taxi!" the scavengers howled.

"No thank you – where does the onward bus depart from?"

"Oh… well… no bus, no bus today…"

"None at all? Not to Jinshangling? Maybe later?"

"Uhh… no… but my taxi is here, just 400 yuan" …

And so on. This continued for quite a while.

Our protests – that we were truly humble travellers – fell on deaf ears. The people sparked into life, and the dollar signs that flashed in their eyes showed why. All we wanted was to take the bus; we genuinely couldn't afford the hundreds of Yuan the taxi drivers were shamelessly demanding. A few of the other Chinese passengers rallied to us, educated perhaps, or just helpful. In vain, they tried to explain to the taxi drivers that we were indeed passing through; not the rich tourist types who had been pouring money into Beijing for the whole month of August. Again and again, our protests fell to the wayside. Eventually, beaten and parched, we gave up. It was mid-afternoon, and the slow realisation that we would not reach Jinshanling set in. The taxi drivers had even rallied around and bullied the government sponsored English-speaking tourist guides into feigning the argument that the buses inexplicably weren't coming that day. Sat in a tent on the corner of the bus station, they couldn't help, and retreated back into their tourism literature. We were outnumbered, and linguistically at a disadvantage. We had one plan; and that was to make a bid for the Badaling section of the Wall before sundown.

We made it, and Badaling didn't disappoint. How did we manage to make it here after all? A mad scramble on the next bus back to Beijing, then across town via subway and on foot, and then another tourist bus out to Badaling made it all possible. It was 6.00 pm, and the sun was beginning to get low in the sky, closer to the foothills. The nearest section of the wall to Beijing city (and subsequently the most touristy) was still visually stunning, and historically fascinating. There were a few gift shops littered around, and quite impressively, a Starbuck's coffee outlet set into one of the walls. The Great Wall's rough stone rises majestically from the earth, almost luring the northern Hordes from bygone dynasties to have a go at conquering it. Winding its way up and around the surrounding hills, you couldn't imagine it not being there. Almost organically, the Wall matches the colours and hues of the surrounding landscape. It is impressive; mighty high and imposing, yet at the same time nestled amongst the shrubs and semi-arid landscape of the Badaling area. Stenciled on the side was a Hollywood-esque board sign commemorating the 2008 Olympics.

Built (and subsequently rebuilt and maintained) between the 5th century BC and the 16th century, the Wall was built primarily to protect China's northern border with Mongolia. Little remains of the most northerly piece of the wall, built between 220 – 206 BC, most of the remaining pieces being built during the later Ming dynasty of the $14^{th} – 17^{th}$ century AD. It stretches over approximately 4,000 miles, winding from Shanhaiguan in the east all the way to Lop Nur in the west of China, traversing in a kind of arc shape along the frontier border of Inner Mongolia. Legend has it that stretches of the Wall contain the bones of most of the 2 – 3 million people who died making it – their grisly final contribution to the state's grandest project.

Craig and I walked for a couple of kilometres along the wall, taking in the watchtowers and the breathtaking views. The long shadows of the wall and its sharp towers stretched across its rural background. We met a Japanese tourist here and talked with her. Yuki was from western Japan, somewhere I hadn't yet spent time. Worldly and quite conversant, she had a professional job back home, and was in town for just a few days. She had bobbed brown hair and wore sporty, loose clothes. Despite it being only a short vacation, she appreciated the freedom other cultures afforded in comparison to life in Japan.

"The culture is too male dominated in Japan" she asserted, "but abroad I feel I can be myself". This theory was something I had heard before from other travelled Japanese.

"Foreign countries aren't as insulated as Japan" Yuki continued; "where it feels as though women must conform".

As we walked along the wall, the thought occurred to me that she probably wouldn't be as forthcoming if we were to have met back in Japan. But she was, and it was refreshing to hear.

The sun was getting lower in the sky. Yuki offered to give us a lift back to the city, in a cab she had hired for the day which was waiting for her. The offer was very, very, gratefully received.

The shadows of the wall grew ever longer into the dusk, and eventually it was time to leave. The yellow taxi we had been bought by Yuki back at the wall weaved in and out of the freeway traffic lanes to the sound of beeping car horns. The dusk of the evening had settled to darkness and what started as a low flicker of light kilometres away gradually turned into the city of Beijing right before my eyes. The city had significantly scaled back its famous pollution emissions for the 2008 Games, and I didn't find its atmosphere unpleasant at all. The light pollution was reasonably noticeable when dark, but in a poetic way it made the City twinkle at night. It was particularly enchanting on the evening of the closing ceremony of the Olympics. The Chinese authorities had put on a staggering event; a very well organised Games which had welcomed foreigners with a minimum of disruption and protest, and the closing night was no exception.

I stood in the Olympic Park, in the north of the city, looking up an avenue to the silver hue of the Bird's Nest stadium, the icon of the Games. The circular metallic structure was lit from within, the glow visible even from where we were stood. The streets were like over-laden sacks heaving and splitting at their seams, almost rupturing with spectators and supporters; the mood was infectious. There was a boisterous hubbub which was very representative of a nation on the edge of its seat, as the defining moment of a generation came to a glorious flourishing finish. Fireworks lit up the sky as the crowd ooh'd and aah'd its way through the evening.

I moved and weaved amongst the crowd, trying to locate a better spying spot until finally the fireworks and music concluded. The humid evening had drawn to a close and the cool midnight air was refreshing after hours walking around the Olympic park. As the pilgrims of this festival of light and optimism dispersed and headed for their trains, I wandered back through a few of the streets to the next-but-one subway station. China was definitely a place I could have killed some time had I had some more opportunity. I did appreciate the civility and wealth of Japan, and the way it appealed to your senses. China on the other hand, was paradoxically at once both a serious and risky place. Things were always in a state of flux, on a macro, cultural level as well as the to-ing and fro-ing on the street day to day, and the people seemed less isolated; rawer in terms of their wants and needs.

***

A couple of evenings whilst I was in Beijing, I took to going to the district of Houhai, north-north west of the Forbidden City. It consisted of a slender, tranquil lake running from north west to south east, surrounded by bars, cafes, and the occasional eatery. Houhai district is also surrounded by great examples of *hutongs* and is a great place to kill time and wander amongst the architectural treats. To the south, the lake continues and turns into Beihai Park, then Zhonghai, and finally into the most southerly Nanhai Lake. Apparently, even Chairman Mao Zedong was drawn to the magnetism of these pleasant lakes, holding court in a compound called 'Zhongnanhai', named after the central and southerly lakes. Trees with droopy, sagging bows surround Houhai Lake, almost shielding it from the rest of the smoky conurbation. In the day, you can rent a boat and go paddle on the lake or visit a traditional tea house on the shore. Night is when the area really comes alive though, when the bars and cafes open up their fronts so you can sit and sip on your beer whilst overlooking the lake. The whole spot is lit by reams of red lanterns, nicely mixed with more modern trendy lighting. It is lively, stylish, and relaxing in tone, making it popular with ex-pats and younger Beijing locals.

Most of the cafes seemed to be competing for the title

of most kitsch interior design. Each successive cafe had brighter colours, more flamboyant cushions, and moodier lighting. Just a few years ago, the area was the habitat of fishermen and park-goers. Now though, since the infamous 'No Name' Bar was opened, which subsequently sparked invigoration in the borough, the neighbourhood has attracted hipper and more upscale clientele. The roads surrounding Houhai Lake have boutiques and more cafes, but take a stroll down the narrower side streets and hidden alleys to find smaller shops, local eateries and rickshaws passing by.

On one occasion I found a place down an alley and behind a shop where a group of locals were eating some traditional stir fried beef, vegetables, and Tsingtao beer. The surroundings were humble plaster, wooden tables, and a few patriotic posters. Rather than paying the highly inflated Olympic-inspired prices, I was able to eat and drink all for under around six Yuan. Here, as in other places in Beijing, I found myself still bowing to people, like I would have done in Japan. It was ingrained in me as a result of having lived there so long. It looked and felt rather stupid, and I always only just realised I was doing it as soon as I had begun.

I had met a friend here in Beijing, a boutique worker called Jinmingxia. Her hair sat in a bob style which was popular here, whilst her trendy clothes hung from her figure. Her large black sunglasses sat snugly on her nose. I had met her in a pub; a friend-of-a-friend of Craig's. Flatteringly, she asked to meet up a few days later. I had a great time with her, even though I didn't really take on board a single word of Chinese. Jingminxia was a long name, so she liked to be called 'Jinx' for short. Suited me fine.

We took in the sites, ambling around the Temple of

Heaven Park (*Tiantan* in Chinese), eating ice cream (delicious), and attempting to learn each other's languages (badly). The Temple of Heaven Park was a lazy place and great for soaking up the culture of the moment, and in that respect was similar to the atmosphere of Yoyogi Park in Tokyo. It was all built by the same Emperor who built the Forbidden City. The buildings there are Taoist, and date to around 1400. The Halls of Prayer and other rich buildings rise up above the leafy, well tendered grassy areas and tall pine trees. The place isn't at all ostentatious though, more respectful than brazen.

People on the grass in the park were doing the usual; sunbathing, playing music, or exercising. One guy was reading a book out loud, in English. He was sweating, shirtless, and his eyes bulging – concentrating hard on his almost unearthly bad performance despite clearly not knowing the first letter of the English language.

Looking up at the Hall of Prayer for Good Harvests, a prime example of the pinnacle of one of the world's greatest civilisations, it was easy to imagine the illustrious empire of former times. The three large storeys which comprise the structure are concentric circles, red walls with a grey roof, and are constructed entirely from wood, with no nails. It gained its name from an annual ceremony of prayer in order to secure a bountiful harvest. As an example of landscape design it was also remarkably inspiring, with delicate tree-lined lawns and an array of flora abounding throughout the 3 kilometre-squared grounds.

We dined on soup near the park, and socialised in the Chaoyang park and Sanlitun entertainment area. We also walked through Tiananmen Square, the biggest public square in the world. At its centre lays the imposing final resting place of Chairman Mao (or the 'Mao-soleum' as it's often jokingly referred to).

Jinx seemed quite familiar with Beijing. I learnt she had studied English at school but years of lack of practice meant she was now worse at it than she had been. As we flittered around and about, I gathered she came from a rural village around two hours bus ride from Beijing, but wouldn't ever consider going back. She said the place was a backwater, relying on the crop farming to stay alive. Her father owned land there and managed to scrape by. But, the way China was developing and progressing; the soaring heights of economic prosperity showed only one thing: that the slow decline of rural areas into decay was paving the way for the future – the ever expanding cities, and the fast march into modernity.

Jinx also took me to a nightclub called GT Banana, where they played funk, house and electronica. The music was great. The place was packed, full to the rafters with young urban types. The whole club was decked out like some kind of spaceship, with brightly lit neon and silver gleaming throughout. At intermittent points throughout the night a pole dancer was lowered from the ceiling, much to the enjoyment of the mass of bodies writhing below. The service was good – this is something the east does very well in general – but the prices were more western than anything I had experienced in China this far. As we left, Jinx pushed her contact details into my hand and asked to know the location of my hotel. Reciting a Chinese address to her whilst drunk was hard, but I managed. In my state I didn't even wonder why she'd asked. Her parting hug was a little lingering, but I pulled away and got into my cab. As the taxi left, I fumbled the piece of paper she had given me into my pocket, and hoped the taxi driver knew where we were going.

A few days later, we ended up in said hotel room as I thought we might. Jinx had come round and found the hotel, although I had no idea she was coming over. We had taken a walk, and when we returned Craig happened to be out. We were sharing pictures and talking in our pidgin *chinglish* about the journey I was on. She flicked through saved pictures on her camera – of her friends; her likes, and dislikes, but also pictures of her home town. The dusty ragged countryside of her birth was a stark contrast to where she lived now. Jinx explained that for as long as she could remember, she had wanted to get away from there. The peasantry of her old life was not for her, if she could help it. It was a sign of the new and ambitious China, I thought. Capitalism, the Chinese way, not as we know it.

Talk began to slow as the afternoon went on. There were silences in our conversation but nothing awkward or unnatural. The day had been humid, so she asked if she could shower. I hadn't anticipated that question but said yes; and she went to the bathroom for a few minutes. Appearing from the steam, Jinx proceeded to pad about my room in just her towel. Her hair was wet and the droplets of shower water ran down her skin. Jinx looked anxious and she made as if she might be inclined to leave. She sat on my bed as she started to gather her clothes and put some things into her handbag.

As she sat there on the edge of the bed, her towel creased slightly and showed glimpses of dark bronze skin, stark against the crisp white of the hotel's finest. She stopped what she was doing and looked up at me. Slowly, she dropped the bag from her grasp, leaned over, and hesitatingly she gave me a peck on the cheek.

The touch of her lips shocked me a bit. Whatever it was, I didn't know. In that moment I wasn't sure I even cared. I kissed her back.

We fell backwards, fumbling and awkward; all broken English and smiles.

It was becoming early evening and to our left, across the hotel room, fading sunlight streamed through the angled wooden-slatted window blinds. The sun began to lower and as the light faded to grey through the window pane the city reincarnated itself once more, the night sky giving birth to a shimmering neon skyline bold against the smouldering dusk and flickering street lights in the smog below it.

Beijing's murky metropolis disappeared behind us as the train track meandered on its voyage through the stunningly pristine landscape of Inner Mongolia, on a course almost due north of the city. We were on a three day sleeper train - Craig and I had opted for a four-berth cabin, but as two bunks were empty, we were left with the cabin to ourselves. This leg of the train journey was on the Trans-Mongolian railway, which in turn connected with the Trans-Siberian.

I stepped out of the cabin into the fairly wide corridor, to catch the view of the scenery rolling by the verge of the tracks. The remarkably bright sunshine we had encountered since leaving Japan was continuing into this leg of the journey, and the rays fell on the dramatic hills of this region in spectacular style. The landscape seemed to be ever-morphing and undulating; from steep-sided quarries full of blasted yellow stone to lush green hills and valleys, eventually turning into the flatter Mongolian steppe. I took photos and videos and hung out the window of the train watching this far-flung part of the world float by. It was amazing to witness the landscape transform before your eyes on a journey of this length. China was a place of immense natural beauty. We were headed through a stunning geographical region of the globe. One section of this route had a road running parallel to the tracks – the railway line through the middle of the valley, whilst the road was higher up the hillside and occasionally ran through tunnels burrowed into the side of the valley. There wasn't much traffic though, the tranquility of the road punctuated only sometimes by intermittent, lonely cargo trucks.

The train we were on was fairly modern, as far as my untrained eye could tell. I had heard that when travelling in Central Asia, the Chinese or Russian trains were the best, whereas the trains from some of the under-developed nations such as Kyrgyzstan were underfunded and generally much shabbier. The other passengers seemed to be a mix of merchants and military types, the former with tons of baggage; the latter on the other hand travelling light. They didn't mix too much with us, but we soon made friends around the *samovar* (hot water dispenser for tea, located at the end of each carriage).

On the second night on board we had to stop at the Mongolian border with China, as the size of the railway tracks differs between the two countries. What this means in reality is that every passenger, accompanied by every piece of luggage, has to depart the train for several hours in order for all the wheels and axles on the train to be changed over. At three o'clock in the morning, this is not the most convenient of rest stops. For the traders, this was their last chance to make a few final purchases to carry over the border. The border was a lonely affair, a true out-post complete with forlorn looking guards and desolate scenery looming in every direction. At this point I noticed the only other foreigners on board, a French couple and an English and American couple. Both were on vacation, having come from the Beijing Olympics and subsequently vacationing on the Trans-Siberian railway to Moscow. They were mildly interested in Craig and I meandering on our course through Siberia, but said they would never consider it for themselves.

The breeze of the late afternoon felt good as I stood at the end of the carriage by the window, leaning out onto the stiff steel windowsill. However, the air was getting chillier – the humid summers of the Orient were making way for the autumnal chills making their way south from the Siberian plain. The lack of humidity was certainly a refreshing change from the summers of Japan and China which were relentlessly muggy. The steppe stretched into the distance; ever boundless. I found the extra sweater I had packed was actually necessary now.

As the sun set to the soundtrack of the gentle rhythmic thump of the carriage passing over the railway sleepers, the long shadows of the swelling hills grew longer into the night.

As the Trans-Mongolian pulled into the suburban shanty towns of Ulaanbaatar, the Mongolian capital, the ragged and fertile autumnal steppe behind us transformed in front of us into a flatter space filled with buildings, cars, and people. The corrugated iron roofs, wooden fences, and outhouses were peppered with splashes of bright colours; walls and tiles were painted blue, green, and pink. Dirty, raw, simple; right from the outset we could see we had arrived in an entirely different place from the security and economic prosperity of East Asia's wealthiest cities.

Horses were milling around the streets, properties were untended, and litter was plainly visible wherever you looked. The poverty was apparent in other ways too; from the train I could see dusty crumbling fences lining the track, which were accompanied by corroded and unused automobiles and a lack of any traffic signs.

So, the Trans-Mongolian leg of the journey was drawing to a close as the train slowly pulled into Ulaanbaatar station, brakes creaking, and slightly late.

I exited the train door with my rucksack slung high over my right shoulder, dropping backwards down the steps three feet or so onto the lower concrete platform.

The ticket office seemed deserted. There was a slight chill to the early evening air. The smoky, hazy city skyline rose above the rail terminal building. Grey concrete high rises complete with imposing Slavic letters printed across the fronts were prominent in the near foreground; the hubbub of car horns emanated from the background. Rusted gates from the front car park led through to the rail platform; the absent ticket barriers proving no obstacle for the mass of people that stood expectantly in front of me.

All the touts from local hostels, hotels, and tourist attractions knew the train timetables and were present with fistfuls of leaflets and phone numbers in hand, scouting for business. They actually outnumbered the handful of passengers who were alighting from the train by about three to one.

Craig and I negotiated with a few for a while, opting for a low budget place we haggled with for a bunk each for three US dollars a night. We walked a couple of blocks across barren grassy plots and eventually hailed a cab.

In Mongolia, every car on the road is a taxi – once you've flagged a car down, the driver may or may not be going your way, and if they're not, they'll probably still take you but just charge a little extra. In a sense, it's a cross between hitching and getting a taxi. It is, of course, completely unregulated and dangerous.

Our cab drove through the centre of town, dropping us off by the apartment block we were staying in. The whole city seemed full of these faceless blocks, remnants of the oppression and uniformity brought in by the Soviets. A few people had tried to break away from this remnant of communism by splashing paint across the walls and sides of apartment blocks; the brightly illustrated murals and colourful images enhancing the space they reside in, if only briefly, a forthright statement of how these people felt about the Soviet legacy.

The lift to get up to the fourth floor was as old as the Soviet-era apartment block it resided in. There was barely room for one adult of medium build; the buttons took an eternity before they finally coughed and whirred into action, and the plastic wood effect trim that ran up the walls may have seemed luxurious in another century. When I told the other tenants here that I had used the lift, their eyes widened immediately, and they gave out troubled warnings. Apparently, that lift had been condemned and could break down at any moment. So, I didn't use it again. Unbeknownst to me, no-one else had used that lift in years.

The hostel was run by a young entrepreneur called Bogey, with her younger sister enlisted as a cleaner and general dogsbody. Bogey had converted her flat into the hostel, and there were two dorms of around four bunks, a double room, a kitchen, and a small bathroom, all accessed through a central corridor. She also laid on a modest breakfast each morning, so every day after I rose in the room Craig and I shared (the other bunks were vacant), I would stand in Bogey's small and tired kitchen, and chomp down the nourishing long-life bread, jam, and black coffee. That combination of a small amount of carbs, sugar and a black coffee got me up in the morning, and it is a breakfast I have relied on regularly ever since. As I did so each morning I was in Ulaanbaatar, I gazed out that kitchen window to the south where the distant, almost intimidating mountains loomed over this grizzled, unassuming city.

***

Ulaanbaatar sits on the Tuul River, a tributary of the Selenge River. The city is just east of the centre of the country, about

4,400 feet above sea level. It may be of interest that it is also the world's coldest capital city, on average. One-fifth of the country's GDP revolves around agriculture, and around 40 per cent of the population still live in the traditional nomadic lifestyle. Twenty per cent of the GDP comes from mining, with the largest gold and copper deposits in the world supposedly under Mongolian soil. Generally a very poor country, times seem to be changing. Mongolia enjoys full democratic ties with most western industrial nations and is trying to turn the economy around. Despite difficulties, the Government remains committed to change. My home country of the UK was the first country to establish these ties with Mongolia in 1990, after the fall of the Soviets. As one of Mongolia's main allies, UK-Mongolia Round Table initiatives on trade, business, and investment, where Mongolia receives valuable economic and political advice, are held every two years.

Despite my earlier impressions of typical life here, the attempts to re-invent the nation's capital are apparent. Tourism is becoming more widespread, and the faces of western backpackers are quite common around town. The presence of middle-class backpackers taking career breaks and gap years from university abounded; we jokingly called them the "North Face crowd" after their penchant for their immaculate designer outdoor wear, which could also mark them out as being 'of means'.

Although trade with China is in decline, the people's quality of life is improving; something attested to by the fact that there are swanky shopping malls popping up around the city centre, offering many western brands of goods and clothing. At that time, there was even a Hilton hotel scheduled to be built. Central Sukhbaatar Square is home to grand government buildings and on the south side of the Square, near Peace Avenue, there sits a curved building which is nearing completion, constructed out of glass and steel. It resembles a ship's sail, the crisp glass and steel rising skyward and curving in the wind. This sail sits serene, looking out over the vast ocean of potential that is Ulaanbaatar, staring peacefully into the middle distance of Mongolia's future.

Nestled away from the centre, towards the north east, is Gandan Monastery, one of only a handful of monasteries which escaped the destruction ordered by Stalin in the 1930s, when Mongolia was still under Soviet control. The place is a Tibetan style Monastery and has a small hamlet of buildings surrounding a grand Temple, housing around 150 monks. The style is uniquely oriental, obviously Asian but still distinctly Mongolian. The edges of the Temple's roofing rise upwards slightly at the end, much like a Japanese pagoda. The white base of the Temple complements the wooden beams and red paint, and the green tinge of the weathered copper roof.

To find the place, walk west on Peace Avenue, and once the shops start to fade away take the long boulevard north. On this approach to the Monastery, I met an English speaking monk who stopped to chat to me about where I was from and where I was going. He stood well over six feet tall, with glasses, and his long burgundy Buddhist robe barely rustling as it flicked along the wide dusty street. The whole time we spoke, his demeanour never faltered from a perpetual smile. His enthusiasm and ease with life was refreshing, and I enjoyed our exchange of pleasantries. He seemed satisfied that I found Mongolia an intriguing culture to visit and saw the value that is ever present in learning about other societies' ways. In a way this monk personified the unquestionable contrast of Ulaanbaatar; his language ability represented the progressive cultural ties that Mongolia has with the rest of the world, whilst his dress and life choice reflected the strong traditions still very much in play in Mongolian society today.

As I continued on into the small settlement, through the imposing gates and bright red paint, the numbers of ambling monks grew larger. The sun-baked walls of the compound radiated orange, cream, and natural verve. The striking serenity of the scene suddenly came to the fore as the sunshine broke through the clouds dispersing beams onto the temple, and a flock of birds slowed, and then silently settled in the courtyard I was taking photographs in. Interestingly, the name of this Monastery ('*Gandantegchinlen'* to give it its full title) means 'Great place of complete joy' in Tibetan, and any visitor will attest to the sheer quietude of the place; a stark contrast to the hum of Ulaanbaatar's downtown department stores. The green of the commanding central temple's battered copper roof sat nicely in the background against the gold leaf roof of the low, square Golden Temple. The colours of these temples, although vibrant and visually arresting, seemed oddly at calm with the light greens and tans of the Mongolian Steppe in the northerly background of the city.

Strolling back around the city centre, just a block or so east of Sukhbaatar Square, lay a blunt reminder of the violent political unrest which dominated headlines about Mongolia over the summer of 2008. Slightly back from the street, to the north, lay a burnt out building with a scraggly patch of grass in front. Broken windows, charred wood, and the black burnt remnants covering the plot were indicative of what happened barely two months before. The 29th June 2008 parliamentary elections precipitated riots which took place on 1st July; mass demonstrations aimed at highlighting the dubious credibility of the election results ended with five people dead and around 50 injured. The elections were deemed credible by the international community; however, the vast majority of the Mongolian population remain skeptical.

Examples of timeless Central Asian culture were to be found in the bazaars that dominate the way people trade in this part of the world, today as ever. In Ulaanbaatar the main bazaar was held on the dusty fringes of the city, amongst empty warehouses and compounds. It was a bus ride away, and we managed to find the right minibus through a little broken Russian. Once you got there, you paid a token amount to enter at the main gate before wandering through endless stalls and shops. The bazaar and the merchants screamed in your face both metaphorically and literally, and offered almost everything you could ever need, but maybe not anything you may actually ever want.

Despite the vast amount of space, these stalls were rivals for space, with goods and merchandise jostling into the walkway and stall owners manhandling both goods and customers. I was in the market for some sturdier shower shoes, and a better insulated jacket in preparation for the upcoming Siberian winter. I had binned the thin, beige, cotton coat I had owned during the Japanese spring – Bogey had seemed to be quite taken with it so I gave it to her, a gift she seemed pleased with. After bartering with the belligerent stall owner for a few minutes, I parted company with US$20 for a Chinese made, genuine-fake North Face jacket. This was to prove a good purchase – whilst not as windproof or well-made as the authentic product, it was a thick layer and extremely waterproof. It was also light and compact, so much so that I was impressed that such a blatant knock off could be useful on this journey. I still own it to this day.

Back in the city later that evening, we found out Bogey had organised a night out at a Mongolian night club for us and the other guests of her hostel. There was a group of guys who had just arrived in Ulaanbaatar after entering the world-famous Mongol Rally, which takes place every year and pits cars against each other in a race with no specified routes whatsoever, as long as you make it to Ulaanbaatar on time. The car you use must have an engine less than 1000cc and you must raise money for charity, but that is it. This group had entered in several cars, but all had encountered mechanical problems and their bangers had failed to finish. They ditched the cars in central Russia and took the train here to Mongolia, to celebrate nonetheless with the other entrants, a symbolic way to mark the journey they'd started.

Again, using the 'hitching-cabs' provided by the locals, the group of about a dozen of us got into about three or four of these 'taxis'. Paying a small fee to enter the club, we soon found ourselves in somewhere quite strange. Like a club anywhere in the world, there was a large dance floor in the centre of the floor, with a bar to the rear, and a stage with a DJ at the front. Tables and seated areas ran up one of the longer sides of the floor. It was dark, as was to be expected, with strobe lights and a disco ball in the centre of the ceiling. So far, so good.

The local beer was cheap enough and the music was all right, house music with the odd recognisable western tune. The local guys however were behaving oddly.

At the sign of the group of us, approximately six or seven white guys, they became very defensive. Passive-aggressive stares across the dance floor turned into direct hostility when we attempted to communicate with the locals. Elbows here and abrasive words there, it was clear we weren't welcome. There were no other foreigners in the club, and due to its out of the way location, I doubt that many had been before. Sat at one of the side tables, we continued to get drunk after leaving the dance floor. Every one of our party commented on the over-protective nature of the men here.

Later in the night, Chris, one of the guys accompanying us from the hostel, stumbled from the gents' toilets claiming he had been the victim of extortion.

He wasn't totally blameless though. I thought at the time it actually seemed like a normal policy. He'd been to the toilets to vomit, after getting really drunk. Unfortunately, he didn't make it in time and had heaved all over some of the night club furniture and all over the bathrooms. The club's owner, claiming the cleaning costs as reason, wanted a large sum of the local currency, the Mongolian Togrog, to let Chris leave the club. Protesting his innocence and getting Bogey involved didn't seem to work. He eventually had to pay, begrudgingly, and we all left for the hostel. As before, a Mongolian hitching-cab took us back to the tower block.

Waking late the next morning, I needed something substantial for lunch to soak up the hangover. Fortunately, we'd found a respectable Japanese restaurant called Sakura in Ulaanbaatar which is run by a Japanese gentleman who moved here and has a Mongolian wife. The place is located about a block away from Peace Avenue to the south. It is quaint and unpretentious, a small building with a white front and concrete steps leading up to the entrance. Inside, there are wooden tables and neat, colourful menus. The gentleman's daughter was our waitress.

"*Irashaimasé*" came the welcome, a familiar term used

to greet customers in Japan.

"*Konnichi wa*", or 'good day to you' was our reply.

"So... where are you from?" came the almost formulaic question, the owner a little surprised at the white people in front of him speaking in Japanese.

We replied, and the conversation grew from there.

It was good to speak in Japanese again, to refresh my memories and not let the language fade. Craig and I talked to the owner briefly but fluently about where we were from, and how he came to be running a restaurant in Mongolia. He wasn't from Tokyo, but from the countryside in Honshu, and had seemingly moved here for his wife and family. Menu-wise, I opted for the *gyu-don*, a simple Japanese meal of fried beef and rice. Also on the menu was *miso* soup, another firm favourite of mine. It's made from seaweed and a few vegetables, and incorporating fish stock, and I used to eat mine with Chinese ramen noodles. I didn't fancy the sushi at a place so far inland, but judging from the rest of the food, the cleanliness, and the customer service, I'm sure it would have been all right.

There were perhaps one or two other customers at the tables, which were a light wood with neat paper table cloths. We didn't really notice them, and it was early evening so it was hard to judge how busy the place could get. The whole meal was more expensive than a backpacker should have been spending on a day-to-day basis, but it was a treat, and good to break the monotony of supermarket food or cheap Russian dumplings. If I ever get the opportunity to return to Ulaanbaatar I would very much like to know if it's still there.

One evening I was walking around the city, and the dusk was slowly setting in. The buildings along the main street mixed from shabby run-down local stores, to shiny cash-injected small businesses. It was a common site that sewers lacked man-hole covers, leaving massive holes in the roads. It was entirely common for people either drunkenly or mistakenly fall down them – to a not very pleasant surprise (and usually an untimely demise). This made it necessary to keep an eye out for the man-holes, as well as the other sites of the city, as you walked along.

Greasy spoon type Russian cafes on one side of the street were contrasted by ice cream parlours and department stores on the other. I felt pleasant. I was heading east towards Sukhbaatar Square after eating a modest meal back at the guesthouse and looking forward to an early night.

Craig was with me, walking about three or four paces in front. I was wearing my new jacket, trainers, and a pair of jeans I had bought in Japan many months previously from a vintage store in Harajuku. Unfortunately, the pockets in the jeans were pretty shallow and didn't leave a lot of room for the wallet. As I walked along the street, I felt a slight slipping sensation in my right jeans pocket. Realising that I was being pick-pocketed I decided in an instant to turn and face the criminal and try to recover my wallet. I turned about and grabbed the young Mongolian guy by the shoulders, the whole movement executed only a split second after I felt my wallet slide away from me. Behind him there were a gang of about four or five similarly turned out teenagers, wearing jeans, hoodie tops and baseball caps.

"Give me my wallet!" I shouted at the youth.

Stunned silence was the reply.

At this point Craig had turned round, wondering why I was shouting in the street. He didn't intervene, instead moving towards me but remaining silent.

The youth struggled and squirmed, trying to get away. His friends could see he wasn't getting out very easily. A few seconds passed before they weighed up the options. One of his mates produced the wallet, throwing it towards my feet.

I didn't notice. The guy I was holding must have passed it back extremely quickly to his mates when I turned.

"Give me my wallet!", I demanded again.

A passer-by who had witnessed the whole thing brought the wallet to my attention.

"Your wallet is there" she said to me calmly, pointing to the tarmac about three feet away from me to my right.

Realising the trade on offer, I let the guy go and stooped to pick up my wallet. I felt very embarrassed. The people on the street had seen me shout at a Mongolian native, even my best friend hadn't a clue what had just happened in the past minute or so, and I had failed to see the gang member throw me the wallet to end the situation. On the other hand, all my cash and cards were in there, and losing it would have been devastating. I had a reserve of cash and traveller's cheques in my rucksack, but organising new cards from my bank and mastercard from Mongolia would have been quite the headache. Acting quickly in this situation had meant the trip could continue. Failing to act would have meant a serious hold up to my plans from a serious financial delay in the short term. I had heard that pick-pocketing was the most common crime here in Ulaanbaatar and that tourists were the prime targets of criminals. This was another reason I felt embarrassed; I am a sensible and grounded traveller who should have foreseen something like this coming.

The young gang all stared at me, briefly, their gaze flickering. Then, composing themselves; they turned and headed down a nearby alley. Craig and I turned back in the direction we were originally heading, our heart beats reduced back to normal levels, and we continued to walk.

Anyway, I thought, as my heart rate reduced, "all's well that ends well".

"Sheesh", Craig said, exasperation written all over his face. No other words were required.

***

Our guides' car travelled across the Mongolian steppe, and a plume of dust trailed from the rear of the beaten-up old saloon. Mongolia and other central Asian countries are large buyers of second hand Japanese and Korean cars, which are imported and then auctioned off at supremely cheap prices. Our four-door non-descript Japanese car made short work of the barely asphalted rural road heading east out of Ulaanbaatar. As well as Craig and I, our translator and the driver made up our team of four.

An hour or so out of the capital, we pulled over in a neatly curvaceous valley between two gently sloped luscious hills. A few feet away, a group of camels congregated in a field, rustically fenced off with wood from the surrounding forests. They grazed and lazed, unperturbed by our presence, underneath the dappled sun shine. Further away, across the road a large *Ovoo* structure sat, the colourful flag atop it flapping in the gentle valley breeze. An *Ovoo* is a shamanistic pyramid structure built of rocks, wood and other debris, as an offering to the Gods. Often, they are colourfully decorated with flags, cloths, and such. Traditionally, you should walk round the structure three times, throwing something onto the pile like a small rock – the belief being that if a person doesn't do this and is thus disrespectful, they will fall ill or die. Craig and I didn't get the chance to see one, but a worship ceremony at an *Ovoo* consisting of monks iterating prayers, people making offerings, and even feasting is a rare but unmissable event.

Craig and I were en route to the Gorkhi-Terelj National Park to see the some of the more breathtaking scenery the Mongolians have to offer. As we headed deeper into the National Park, the gentle sloping hills of the morning gradually morphed into the dramatic cliff faces of the afternoon as we speed on eastwards. The Turtle Rock on the western side of the Park is a giant erosion formed rock resembling a turtle, rising dramatically out of the brown sandy landscape, visible from quite a distance as we approached. A nimble and slim individual could slip into the large crevice near the base and attempt to climb up nearer to the head of the turtle, grasping and clutching at the rock face, scrambling.

Later, as the sun began to descend, the deep red shimmering over the dramatic heights of the luscious green mountain ridges, the tyres of our ride crunched into the rich khaki dirt road. To our left stood another eroded pillar of stone, easily four times the height of the Turtle Rock we had negotiated earlier that day. Touts selling horse and camel rides were doing their business, although as the dusk loomed their sales began to fade. Craig and I, accompanied by our enthusiastic translator, again clung to the jagged rock face to gain a higher viewpoint across another spectacularly green valley. We had come at the right time of year, the summer had ended, yet the winter had not yet set in. The autumn had its frostiness – even a little gloom in the air – but it was nothing compared to the big freeze of the Mongolian mid-winter that loomed beyond our stay. The twilight of the dusk was bright; as we made for camp it cut right through the shadows that were creeping across the valley floor into the night.

The Ger we were camped in was situated on the edge of a Mongolian Ranch, owned by a family that Bogey our landlord back in Ulaanbaatar knew. The farm was in the bottom of a valley, surrounded by sparse forest, whilst the Ger camp was situated beside a small murmuring brook – our source of water for washing for the duration of our stay. The brook winded round two of the edges of our camp and was crossed by two felled trees that worked as primitive bridges. The circular tent that the four of us would occupy was centred on an Aga-style cooker and fire in the middle, with a vent in the top for the smoke to ascend from. The wooden beds (far too short for a tall well-fed tourist to stretch out in comfortably) were brightly painted, orange, red, and green and were positioned around the lower edges of the tent.

In the next Ger, an Italian named Johnny and his colleague were also travelling through, not forward to Russia like us, but vacationing here in Mongolia before heading back to Turin in a few weeks. Our hosts served us traditional Mongolian barbecued meat, tender and tasty, as well as yoghurt, biscuits, and sweet tea to snack on. As we ate underneath the boughs of the autumnal woodland Johnny and his quieter companion chatted to us in their decent command of the English Language, gained whilst travelling the world. Johnny had been to over 100 countries, across all the continents, and lived to travel; he was fortunate enough to have a flexible job which allowed him weeks or months off at a time. The pair were curious about our journey, and slightly jealous we had the time to wind our way home rather than fly back. We sipped a couple

Tokyo sprawl

Shibuya

Hachiko crossing

Chopsticks

Tokyo reflections

This city never sleeps

Taking a ride in Yokohama

Yokohama

Decent powder is an easy drive from Tokyo

Matcha tea – emotional support dog optional

Nikko

I still count Craig as a great friend. He's always smiling.

The actual Slow Boat to China

Southern Japanese coast in the background

The Beijing 'Bird's Nest' national stadium

The Forbidden City

The 'Maosoleum'

Americans ...

'One World, One Dream'

Yes, you are right. I am cooler than you.

Badaling

The train to Ulaanbaatar

Ulaanbaatar, from the kitchen window

Outside the Gandan monastery

Rural Mongolia

An Ovoo

'Brokeback'

Mongolia is one of most stunning places I've ever been

Downtown Ulaanbaatar

Smoking ruins

Street life

'Down time'

Candles at Gandan

of tinned Mongolian beers late in to the night, and at one moment as I looked up into the sky, the thought occurred to me that I might never see a starry sky as crisp, clear, and bright as the one I was looking at right then.

I rose at dawn, stooping to exit from the flamboyantly painted wooden door at the front of the Ger. These distinctly Central Asian structures are semi-permanent, being transportable but still robust and fixed. The wooden frame comes down in panels, which all slot together in a circle, and in turn support the angled roof beams. The canvas then sits over the whole frame, and the tent will sit in place for a season or two. Then, when the weather changes or if the nomadic urge sets in, the whole lot fits into a horse drawn cart for transportation across the rocky windswept steppe.

Mottled rays fell through the leaves of the forest, by now slightly curling and browning at the edges, and I followed the brook along its curving path, crossing at crude temporary bridges made by felling a log across the water, or other convenient places. Some of the ground was boggy and lush with thick grass, but all of it was blessed with such rich trees and plant life. I initially thought I was walking in sedate silence, but as the sun rose ever so slowly, so increased the birdsong and other background natural sounds we all take for granted.

I soon came across another camp of Gers, but the inhabitants hadn't risen yet. The sun was now fully up, and the owners' dog was barking and fooling around in the dirt. This camp had more facilities than ours; a nicer outdoor toilet as opposed to a hole in the ground in a shed, as well as more tables and land. Today we had plans, so after a while of observing the scene and the owners not rising, I meandered back the way I had come to our own Ger to find the others also getting out of bed.

The allure of trekking a few kilometres across the steppe of Mongolia using horses was an easy one to give in to. The owners of the Ger lent Craig and I two horses to ride on, on the condition that a guide from the camp rode with us and guided our horses – neither of us were competent riders, and for the most part my animal was quite stubborn. I had returned from my saunter through the forest and after sipping on some sweet black tea and having eaten some doughy bread and yoghurt, the both of us mounted up and started the trek up the hill and over the ridge to the plains beyond. Although autumn was upon us, and we had left the humid heat of the Far East firmly behind, Mongolia was still lush and far greener than I ever thought possible. The horses plodded on across the vast plain – horizon was all that you could see – and occasionally stopped to nibble at a plant or tree. The route seemed to curve, as our guide would take the three of us almost zig-zagging up the extreme edge of the steppe, where there was a ridge which in turn gave way to more of the steppe on the other side. The steppe was like a very shallow valley, slight curves rising up to another small ridge to the extreme right of our perspective. In some ways I find it similar to the Great Plains of central Canada; undulating but flat at the same time, weirdly. We made slow progress; but no matter, time was immaterial at this point. The gentle plod of the horses was pleasant, no more than a man's jogging pace, but sometimes we might pick up speed. We eventually cantered back down to the lowland. The steppe was fertile and in some areas a bit boggy. Slowly we came across a ford, a river running through the middle of this seemingly limitless ground. On the other side of the crossing lay a small hamlet, again, traditional in nature. Small dirt tracks led into the settlement, which was characterised by these same small shacks you find all over Mongolia; these structures all ramshackle whilst simultaneously giving off an air of complete permanence. Perhaps it was just the ruggedness and romance of it all, but they seemed as if they'd be completely impervious to the elements despite only being made from wood, corrugated iron, and limited brick work. And, just like the suburbs of Ulaanbaatar, some of these houses had been painted in a variety of colours – pastels, pinks and light blues.

A passing local offered his compliments as we passed – our guide returned hers and we did the best we could to return ours.

The nomadic way of life here is shrouded in romance, but it is important to note the origins of the word. 'Nomad' comes from the Greek nomos, meaning 'pasture'. A nomad proper is therefore one who tends to his domesticated animals. Rather than the farmer who must stay in one place and tend to his crops, the nomad must go where his flock goes, and tend to them in that way. Without this movement, they would die. A nomad therefore does not roam aimlessly, nor are nomads hunters either. Both of those descriptions miss the central tenet of the nomadic existence. The steppe here cannot support crops, but it can support livestock as long as they keep moving. So too must a nomad support the animals and plot his or her movements along this seasonal path – to be at one with the land and the flock, as well as their horse, in order to not merely survive: but to exist.

My horse was by now becoming even more stubborn, and quite frankly I had had enough. The animal's grey skin looked old, neglected even, and I supposed it must have been a working animal for many years. Our guide insisted we swap, a sentiment indicated through signs and gestures, as neither of us knew each other's languages. Her horse had a glossy brown coat, a black mane, and seemed younger with more dash in its step. Swapping worked in the short term, and the guide managed to coax a slow trot out of my old horse. We passed the settlement and headed out again across the plain, picking up speed and passing through the lowland and scrub until we reached a patch of trees which offered a decent place for the horses to rest and get some shade and take on water. Reaching this far, the guide decided we should turn back in the direction we had trekked and headed back to camp. We took a more direct route back on some of the higher ground, missing out the village but still able to see it a few miles away in the distance. On the way in, the gathering clouds appeared, and a light rain set in. I was wearing trainers, jeans, and my newly-acquired fake jacket. The jacket did well against the rain, it was the first time it had been road tested and I was pleased.

Back in Ulaanbaatar, it was our last night in the city before we had arranged to push on into Russia. Italian Johnny and his mate joined us for a night out with a few others from the hostel, as well as Bogey and some of her friends. It was at this point that I discovered that a lot of the Mongolian words I'd learnt were completely useless. People did not get Craig's or my pronunciation. We were puzzled as to why and were pondering it with Johnny and the rest of the group. After a while Bogey interjected and informed us that her sister, who had been our main teacher of a few bits and pieces of the language, had a really strong lisp – and so we were mis-taught in the first place..! Craig found this especially funny.

As previously alluded to, the city does have a few decent restaurants, mixing it up with traditional grills and barbecues through to Indian tandooris, steaks and there's even an Irish pub. We were eating somewhere modest and sat around the small tables in a dimly lit and otherwise sparsely filled restaurant. Bogey said she would miss us, and Johnny talked about how his job loomed, the prospect of going back to Italy not surprising – but a bit sad that his holiday was over. The Mongol rally guys agreed. The past few months had been like another life for a lot of them, now returning to their jobs and the lives they had before.

Just a few blocks away lay the wealthy shopping centres and the under-construction Hilton hotel that symbolised a new, globalist Mongolia. The 'North Face crowd' of gap year backpackers were around too, to be found in the shops, markets, and bars of this city. Maybe Johnny and the gang weren't returning to anywhere markedly different from here, after all.

Crossing the Mongolian/Russian border had many similarities with crossing from China into Mongolia. The culture was definitely becoming more European, less Asiatic, and the Cyrillic writing on billboards and signs was becoming more common. The weather was also turning, and the sluggish summer in Tokyo seemed an eternity ago compared with the overcast skies and dropping temperatures Russia was presenting. More and more Caucasian faces populated the streets, and more people attempted to talk to us about our journey. No longer were the dishes served to us Ramen noodles, or Chinese dumplings, but now they were traditional Central Asian and Russian staples such as the *beefsteaks*, a sort of patty made from minced beef, or *pelmeni*, the indigenous Siberian bland dumplings which you had to heavily season with pepper. Also on offer was a dish fundamental to Russian culture, *borshch* soup. This beetroot soup was served with a splattering of sour cream on top (in most places) and with some dense traditional bread. If you were lucky, or Russian, you washed it down with vodka. I loved *borshch*, it was simple, delicious, and almost every cafe in Russia served it. Although it's Ukrainian in origin, the Russians add cabbage, and sometimes potato to the mix, and I sometimes had varieties with meat in too. *Borshch* and *Pelmeni* proved to be my staple throughout late 2008, and I noted that Russian cuisine was hearty and nourishing.

I was sat on a rickety bus on my way out of Ulaanbaatar headed for Ulan-Ude, a pleasant city over the border in Siberia. It is famous for having the largest sculpted head of Lenin anywhere in Russia, a towering 7.7 metres tall and weighing in at a hefty 42 tons. Ulan-Ude was originally inhabited by Mongols and the Evenks, a northern Russian indigenous people; in 1666 the Cossacks arrived and founded a fortress, calling it Udinsk. The area was an advantageous geographical area, and as such the old town flourished from trade with China and Mongolia. The Trans-Siberian railway came to the city in 1900, and after a few name changes it was finally re-named Ulan-Ude in 1934. It's the third largest city in Eastern Siberia, and there are old buildings here along the river bank which serve as excellent examples of Russian classic architecture. Since leaving Ulan-Ude, I read that in the city pairing scheme, Ulan Ude's twin is nearly exactly opposite it on the Earth's surface, meaning Puerto Natales in Chile is nearly exactly antipodal to it. And although now the city welcomes foreigners, with cinemas, bars, supermarkets, and internet cafes flourishing, it was hard to believe it was actually closed to foreigners until as late as 1991.

The ride on the bus was firm, and the bus really only a budget option on a route only used by the rag and bone merchants who frequent this part of the world. However, despite the cooler temperatures and dashes of rain, the scenery was breathtaking. The lush plains of Mongolia gave way to the darker evergreen tones of a densely wooded Siberia, thick with rich brown silty mud tracks and small streams swelling higher as the prospect of winter drew tantalisingly nearer. The bus struggled up the rough off-road hill tracks, but never faltered. More and more villages were visible as the journey progressed through this fertile Siberian wilderness, and soon I could see Ulan-Ude appear in the distance. Passengers on the bus seemed astonished by our presence:

"Why are you travelling on this bus?" they asked.

"We're going home", I replied.

"So… where is your hometown?"

"*Velika Britannia*" – "It's in Britain" I responded, aware of recent diplomatic arguments between our two countries.

"You are a tourist? Why not fly?" they persisted.

"I'm not a tourist. I'm here to see your country, from the ground" I would offer.

"This is a poor, deprived place" was often the local view of Siberia. The people always added "there is nothing to see here", with a firm dose of humility.

The pursuit of travel for its own merits and satisfactions was a strange concept in these parts, and it was unfortunately not to these people's satisfaction that I continued to answer their questions about my trip, and crucially my motivation. Behind their genuine surprise and mild disdain lay a curiosity which lies at the root of most people's minds the world over, so it was not hard to forgive the pointed phrases and cold looks; to smile, and try to be the most diplomatic ambassador I could be.

The bus dropped Craig and I in a street several blocks from the Central Square. I was impressed with my initial impressions of the town and it had a real sense of cultivation about it. Trees and greenery abounded, and it didn't appear to have as many of the brooding Soviet tower blocks as Ulaanbaatar did; the type that seemed so dark, so devoid of light, they could only have been some sort of Soviet-conceived project to create an architectural black hole.

A tram system ran through the city, which was a convenient aspect of this city I wasn't expecting and gave off a cosmopolitan atmosphere to the first town in Russia I encountered. My first impressions stuck.

We had unsuccessfully tried to get a room for the night in one of the guesthouses in the city. The evening drew near, and after that we'd been all over town to various other guesthouses, calling at places and knocking at doors, alas to no avail.

Our last resort proved to be a winner though. We had the number of a Polish 'Culture House' situated a few blocks from the city centre and a short walk from the rail stations. Whilst admiring the massive Lenin head in the central square, Craig and I had gotten chatting to a Vietnamese-German girl who was studying Polish here in Ulan-Ude. It was she who mentioned they took people, and gave us the number of the Culture House just in case. And, what a life saver that number turned out to be.

Culture houses were set up to promote and educate people as to a particular culture, and in this particular house Polish nationals living in Ulan-Ude could congregate, learn, play music, and study amongst peers. It was a nice idea and reasonably common in Eastern Europe and Russia, but I'd never encountered one before. We telephoned the owner, and as always Craig's command of Russian secured us a meeting. We met the owner, Svetlana at the Culture House, hoping she would provide us with some lodgings for our stay. She was initially a little apprehensive that we weren't actually Polish, but I think Craig threw in a few Polish words here and there, and we both professed a great love of Polish cuisine and culture. After a little more persuasion the apprehension turned almost 180 degrees; she was beaming, happy for us to stay in fact, and almost batted away talk of money as inconsequential. In the end we paid her a few dollars a night whilst we were in town.

We chatted, and the smiles and peasantries abounded. There were no available guest rooms, all being occupied by Polish students and musicians. We could however have the floor of one of the music rooms, if that modest, bare floor would suffice?

We had little option: of course, it would do.

The room we had was basic and chilly – but not down at heel in any way. There was a piano in the corner, and a few chairs in the room. The polished wooden floor lay bare and there was a decent sized window on the far wall. As there were no beds, Craig and I used the chairs as a makeshift bed; lining them up in sufficient length to sleep outstretched on. We took it in turns each night – one person on the 'bed', the other on the floor, using bundled clothing as a pillow.

One of the Polish residents, Albert, offered to show us around the city. We had made quite the impression with the other guests here; they were curious about us in any number of ways.

We weren't Polish? Where then were we from? How did we find ourselves here? How long will you be here? Are you learning Polish? What do you think of Russia? Do you like Ulan-Ude? Did you meet Polish people in Japan? Where are you going next...?

Amongst all these questions and good-natured conversations, we met Albert. He spoke English as well as Russian and seemed a man of his word.

Albert was a Polish student, studying Russian and music. He seemed to have an innate love of culture and was expressive about Russia and the history of Ulan-Ude. I felt we would learn a lot about this region from him, and whilst we learned some more Russian, he took the opportunity to practise his English.

"There's not loads to do, but I can show you the city", he enthused one morning.

Naturally we took him up on the offer. We walked through the pedestrianised city centre where western brands and retail stores were still open in the late afternoon. A Gap, a Nike shop, and an Adidas store all populated the main street. I was surprised to learn that they could operate a business in this area, but there were two aspects of this display of western consumerism that I learnt from Albert; firstly that although they seemed affluent, most people in Ulan-Ude probably couldn't afford the merchandise on offer; and that also, more importantly, these stores symbolised the rise of a democratic and unashamedly capitalist Russia. The sign of things to come, perhaps.

The city planners of Ulan-Ude had done a good job. The trams were on time, the buildings were pretty, and the central district was littered with fountains, plaques, and seemed safe to walk through at night. Outside in the suburbs though, many houses were made of wood, and seemed untended and unkempt, even derelict in some cases. I guess the contrast bore a nod to the Ulan-Ude that existed before Russian capitalism, closed to the outside world, a more traditional and explicitly insular city.

We all stopped for a bite to eat, and ate pizza at a second storey fast food place overlooking the city's main street. I think it was part of a mall or cinema or something.

"The Culture House is a good scheme" Albert started, out of nowhere.

"I get to study and live somewhere different, with likeminded people".

Apparently, the other Polish residents agreed, and wanted the scheme to flourish.

"What do you think of the Russians?" I asked.

Albert paused for a while and stopped eating, considering his words. After an age, he replied, very succinctly.

"The Russia of today is very... different", he said, staring straight ahead, as if deep in thought.

And, like that, he took another vigorous mouthful of pizza, munched it down, and turned away to look at a poster on the wall.

We let Albert's statement linger as he chomped away, deep in thought, for a brief period of time seemingly unaware of us or anything else around him.

Later that week, as I walked alone, I came across a Russian Orthodox church near the city's bus station. The orb-like spires common on Russian places of worship, shimmering bright blue and white, rose up from an otherwise ordinary part of the city. Two grizzled old 'salt-of-the-earth' type *babushkas* sat basking outside, blankets in their laps.

"*Dobreya ootra*" (good morning) I offered.

"*Dobreya ootra*" they returned; smiling, slightly amused at the sight and sound of a foreigner.

The grounds of the church were untended, and it looked as if no-one had been there in months. However, the patchy grass and flaking paint of the railings were no distraction from the splendid structure in front of me.

Inside, the church was immaculate. The stained glass of the walls shone brightly and the stone floors had recently been swept. High up was the Russian Orthodox crucifix symbol, similar to the cross we know in the west, but with two angular lines through the top bar. The temperature seemed unnaturally cold, and near the front pew there was an elderly Russian woman wrapped up warm, praying. You could pay a donation for a candle, light it, and say a prayer. Not being religious, I didn't bother. However others had, and the whole place was lit with the subdued light of a hundred candles. The ceiling was high, and the light colour of the sandy interior stone added to the feeling of cold. Religious artefacts from the past were displayed in glass cases on the lobby walls, a well-presented reminder of the history and culture of the Russian Orthodox church. A few people milled around these cases, locals who had come to pay penance or pray, I imagine.

I wandered outside and across the road. Stopping to get refreshment from a street vendor parked up at a car park near a bus station, I ordered a drink.

Chai c molokom" was how I liked it, *pazhalusta* – 'if you please'.

Tea, with milk. In Russia the tea is served black and sickly sweet. Often the old *babushkas* will offer you honey instead of sugar. But, in these parts the addition of milk is a luxury you pay extra for.

Ulan-Ude seemed to offer a lot to its residents. The place was calm and pleasant. I'm sure that as winter drew on, it would probably get a lot more uncomfortable, but when I was there, I was impressed.

For now, Craig and I had tickets booked on the three-day sleeper train to Vladivostok. The route went solely through Russian territory, going northwards, then east and south again around the area of Chinese Manchuria which bulged into Russia's borders. At the station, we toyed with the idea of paying for a minibus, or *mashrutka* to Sludyanka, a town a little further east into Siberia, before feeling uneasy with both the driver's demeanour and the intended routes. This was still a harsh area of the world, and the Russian people are amongst the least respectful of human life I have ever met. I can only guess it is a product of an unforgiving upbringing, born of poverty and corruption.

Once on the train, as a passenger you settle into a humble bunk, with four beds to a berth and a small table in the middle. There are two beds on each wall, with about five or six berths perpendicular to the corridor running down the carriage. It was similar to the train I had caught out of Beijing; however on this there were no doors or solid walls separating the berths; it was like a long dorm room. At the end of each carriage was a *samovar*. The bedding seemed to be changed every day or two by a maid who sat in a room opposite it; she also sold potato crisps, bread, tea bags and sugar – everything a growing boy needs.

Opposite Craig and I, completing the berth, were a large Russian military non-commissioned officer, and a soldier. The soldier was burly, short but stocky. He wore a striped long sleeve t-shirt which looked like it was military issue, and he had slim pyjama bottoms on and plastic shower shoes. The NCO was balding and often sat without a shirt on at all, revealing his hirsute back and belly. He wore a wedding ring on the third finger of his right hand (not left, as was the custom in Russia), and had several gold teeth I gleaned sight of through the odd wry smile and mischievous cackle. He rarely spoke to us but seemed amiable. As the two entered the carriage the soldier squashed his lunch against his luggage by accident, which squirted tomato juice down his trousers. He cursed under his breath as he brushed the pips and juice off himself.

The soldier identified us as foreigners and began to talk with us. He was suspicious at first but eased up as Craig and I endeared ourselves to both him and the NCO.

He taught me a bit of Russian and was polite enough to call me a fast learner.

As we talked over our three-day journey, we gathered the soldier was a seasoned professional in this business of arms, having served all over Russian territory, the Caucasus, the Balkans, and Afghanistan. He hailed from Chita in east Siberia and was a game hunter by trade. He was very cool, confidently talking with us about our trip. The soldier effected surprise that we had lived in Japan but didn't question us further about life there. Again, as I had experienced prior on this trip, the concept of travel for cultural reasons was alien to him, and conversation topics pleasingly consisted of: our experience of Russia, Russian girls, and vodka, not always in that order.

Later, back in England, I calculated that for every day I spent in Russia I had drunk a half of a bottle of vodka, a statistic which started on this very train. We drank vodka with every meal, including breakfast. Even if lunch was a spot of salad and sweet tea, the bottle would be opened, and we wouldn't stop until it was empty. Empty? No matter – the train stopped every 12 hours or so at a local station where more rural *babushkas* sold potatoes, vegetables, sausages and home-made vodka so strong it could blind you, littering the station platform with stalls, bottles, and baskets. You didn't even have to get off – they'd come right up to the windows. As it happens, Russian sausage, salad vegetables, and a spot of vodka wasn't an altogether bad meal.

When it wasn't meal time, we drank just as much, as card games and conversations both warranted vodka-consumption of similar proportions. The Russian word '*davai*' (roughly 'come on' in English) was used in almost all situations and especially ones like these, where a strong stomach was called for.

"*Sto gram, davai*!": ('100 grams, come on!' – the standard unit measure in these parts!) was the cry that resounded, reminding us to drain the glass and continue with the fun. I found that despite their reputation, the Russians were more careful with their drink than we British. We have a world-renowned reputation for drinking to excess, but most Russians I met always balanced their consumption with food, snacks, or moderated it with water or breaks in drinking. So, despite the volume, this method negated a 'binge' culture that might otherwise exist.

However, all that drinking sure made the journey more

tolerable – and certainly more enjoyable. One such stop was at the town of Belogorsk, just north of the northern tip of Manchuria. The situation was dire: we were out of booze and action was required to remedy this stark turn of events. Adding to the complex problem; we had just ten minutes before the train would depart. Leaving Craig and the Officer with our stuff, the soldier and I made a mad dash across town to a supermarket that the soldier knew from having been here before. The jog took us five minutes and as we rounded the corner, our faces fell as we realised the shop was closed. We had just five minutes before the train doors would close but didn't want to go back empty handed. We saw our opportunity and ran – a small newspaper kiosk in the street, like a toll booth in size, where the occupier sold snacks and drinks from a small window in the side. They didn't stock alcohol, but we had to return with something. Having made it there in a few bounds, stocked up on bread, snacks, and soda drinks, we dashed back across the town centre to the railway station. Racing up the platform, we swung onboard just as the whistle blew to signal the locking of the doors, and our onward departure. Panting, we fell to the floor, backs against the walls of the carriage with relieved smiles, our spoil ready to be divided amongst the four of us.

After a pause of a few seconds, the NCO's head popped round the seats. The pair of Russians exchanged a glance and the NCO piped up, with a smile slowly broadening across his face, a glint in his eyes. I knew what was coming but sure wasn't going to be the one to explain the lack of vodka to him.

"....Sto gram... davai?!"

The railway track curved its way around the bay into Vladivostok. It is easy to see why it is named Vladivostok – the

'Lord of the East'. The surrounding scenery is lusher than in Siberia, with the bright greens, fertile trees and rolling coves giving out to the crisp Sea of Japan.

The whole city dominates the local area, sitting on the end of the Muravyov-Amursky peninsular across the Zolotoy-Rog or Golden Horn bay (named for a similar bay in Turkey, apparently). It is the foremost Pacific Russian city, culturally and economically. Central to this city is the railway station, which sits comfortably down by the waterfront. The familiar sound of creaking brakes and hissing hydraulics accompanied the even more familiar feeling of checking my backpack before climbing down onto yet another train platform.

As we exited the station the soldier we had journeyed with wished us a pleasant stay in Russia and enquired where we were staying. Satisfied we would survive, he turned and walked off into the bustle, melting into the Vladivostok crowds, never to be seen again. I have only one regret from this trip, that we should have spent more time with this modest soldier whilst we had the opportunity. Afterwards Craig and I thought we should have offered to buy him a few beers on our first night in town, as way of a thank you. We stood there contemplating this, whilst the stiff coastal breeze ridded us of the cobwebs built up over 76 hours spent inside a train, largely dehydrated.

Known as the city of 'sea-cucumber cliffs' in Chinese, Vladivostok and the surrounding area had been a part of many different Chinese states over the years until it was acquired by Russia by treaty in 1860. Like a lot of Russian cities Vladivostok has a tram and trolleybus as part of its excellent public transport and has a rather charming funicular too. Famous Vladivostok alumni include the actor Yul Brynner, and the military officer Stanislav Petrov, the man credited with averting nuclear war with the USA in 1983 after a malfunctioning early warning system went off – and he disobeyed orders to retaliate.

Wandering uphill from the train station, we searched the hills of the surrounding neighbourhoods of Vladivostok for a hostel. Luckily, we had all day and the weather was warmer in these parts. After finding nowhere suitable, we decided to spend a little on a hotel, and opted for a reasonable place a few streets away from the railway station. The room was satisfactory, complete with two double beds and western TV channels.

The town however had much to entice us out of the semi-luxury of the hotel. The waterfront, replete with ice cream stands, calm waters, and bronzed Russian girls earned itself the name of 'Shashlik beach' due to the abundance of *shashlik* stalls there. The dish is a basic kebab, skewered meat, and although the name is Turkish in origin, it is a firm favourite throughout the former Soviet bloc.

The beach, this Russian Riviera if you will, with its bars, *shashlik* places, and exuberant atmosphere was a location of choice for local young people who hung out and let their hair down in the warming autumn sun. The latest pop songs blared out from beat-up old stereos on the beachfront (the type that still had two tape decks on the front) and it seemed the most European place I had been to in the best part of two years. The reality of course, was that in fact we were facing the Pacific Ocean, on the eastern tip of Russia, ironically having gone back a time zone as we travelled further towards our start point in Japan. The climate was also quite different to the one we had left in Ulaanbaatar a week previously. The days were much warmer whilst the only chill came with the coastal winds brought on by the clear sunset over the bay. In a way, it seemed like the one parting shot at summer before we had to depart for the colder, wintry climes in Siberia in the weeks to come.

The town is also the home of Russia's Pacific Naval fleet, something which dominates the demographic of the city as well as the panorama of most of the harbour. The fleet can be seen from the high ground which overlooks the bay, or just as impressive, from ground level by their moorings. The region of which Valdivostok is the capital, the Primorsky region, literally translates as 'maritime territory' and the sea plays an important part of the city's history. Echoing the history of Ulan-Ude, Vladivostok was closed to foreigners until 1991, but prior to 1958 was a major player in international trade, being a hub for Chinese, Japanese, Korean and American traders hailing from places such as Yokohama and San Francisco.

It was whilst I was in Vladivostok that I became aware of the way in which Russian cafes operate in the majority of cases. Despite having menus chock-full of choice dishes from all over the former Soviet empire, more often than not the owner will have one dish to serve, until they next re-stock. Sat at a typical Russian cafe in Vladivostok, the unusually smiley waitress came over to take our order. The plastic chair creaked a little, and the flimsy table covered in a paper table cloth reminded me of the type you see at beaches all over cheap holidays to Spain. The menu was largely Georgian but I opted for the *beefsteaks*. After having my order refused several times as the cafe had none of that left, it occurred to me to ask what they did have to offer, at which point the waitress became far more receptive and hospitable. Most cafes in this region operated the same way – supply and demand dictates. You ate what they had in, rather than what you would choose to eat. This simple way of bartering often meant that I lived on *borshch* throughout my time in Russia (this time included), but the food was for the most part delicious, and I enjoyed the randomness of it all.

Yet another form of transport, and this time it was water-borne. A hydrofoil to be exact. Craig and I were on course for Komsomolsk-na-Amure, bound from Kharbarovsk, a pleasant city just 30km from the Chinese border. The deep cerulean waves of the river lapped the hydrofoil's wings and the shore which surrounded the river was full of rocks, patchy grassland, and scraggly, desolate trees. A couple of people on the boat identified us as foreigners.

A simple "*Zdrastvootye*", or 'hello', was all I could muster.

The journey to Komsomolsk-na-Amure would take seven hours, and the seats on the crowded hydrofoil weren't exactly comfortable. How I had managed to get to these uncomfortable circumstances, and quite why I was so particularly uncomfortable, I will go into.

Rewind a few days, and I was in Khabarovsk. The best thing about Khabarovsk, and the first thing you notice about the city, is the wide Ussuriskaya Boulevard stretching for eons from the suburbs right up to the jewel in the boulevard's crown, the Orthodox Transfiguration Cathedral in the central Komsomol'skaya Square. Like all Orthodox churches, the architecture is striking; a mix of grandiose frontage and ornate spires. The white of the walls and window frames dazzled in the late autumn sun and were complemented by the gleaming crucifixes adorning each spire. The red brick of the cathedral echoed throughout many of the other buildings in Khabarovsk.

A stone's throw from Komsomol'skaya Square lays the Amur River and waterway network; and, strangely, lining the river are sandy beaches, sun loungers, and ice-cream parlours more akin to Mediterranean climes than the river bank of a rural, northern Russian town.

At this time of year, the river promenade takes on another identity, relishing in the sunshine and the last waves of humidity as summer draws to a close. Beer tents nestle along the promenade, dubbed 'mushrooms' by the locals due to their temporary, seasonal capacity – the fact that they spring up at this time of year before dying out in colder weather. Complementing these tents are ice cream joints, and stages for live music. There is an almost child-like feel of delight in the air, a mood compounded by the teeming beach, bursting with sunbathers despite the nearest coastline being 300 kilometres away. Not many ventured into the river though; the waters are still dangerously close to the heavily polluting industries which line the river out past the suburbs.

The people in Khabarovsk seemed very sociable, and never did I feel unsafe, even at night. Most wanted to practise their English, and some even continued to teach me to drink 'Russian style'. At one point I met a local girl, going to local restaurants with her and later to a beer garden. Lina, a blonde, wore large dark sunglasses and attempted the sultry and cold, unattainable look so many Russian women aspire to. I thought that her style smacked more of being dissatisfied, but I did like the company and our flawed attempts at conversation. We got to talking down by the river over ice cream and took it from there. She had a friend – Valeriya, a brunette, who was much more at home with English speakers; could she join us?

Valeriya was a different fish entirely: expressive and engaging, smiling often, and flicking her long brown hair back behind her ear and adjusting her top. Lina did have a cheeky twinkle to her blue eyes, it must be said, whilst Valeriya's innocent brown eyes oozed with questions and expressions.

We sat in a bar on Muravyov-Amursky Street, drank reasonably cheap vodka, and chatted. Lina worked in a shop and Valeriya, the third wheel, was a student at the local university.

"The Far East isn't considered to be Siberia", Valeriya explained in rushed Russian, "we have a different cultural identity and geography".

She continued, gesticulating aimlessly with her hands as her eyes darted about the room. She was getting more excited about proving we weren't in Siberia, even though I clearly understood and agreed with her.

"Siberia is very remote, it's the interior. Kharbarovsk, here in the east for example, is more European. It's more accessible and civilised".

My experience so far led me to concur. The people of Vladivostok and the neighbouring Krais, or boroughs, saw their evolution as very European as opposed to Asiatic.

The beaming smile she displayed showed a happiness at practising her English and making such a good job of it. In turn, Valeriya taught me some more vocabulary in Russian, as did Lina. I began to enjoy their company a bit more, so I faked not being able to say certain things in Russian so they'd continue to teach me in their breezy, flirtatious manner.

***

I had managed to pick up a rather debilitating stomach virus, possibly from some dodgy food in Vladivostok, but resolved to destroy the bug through a cunning regime of vodka drinking - enough of the local 100-proof alcohol would get rid of the thing, I asserted, even if only to myself. I wasn't letting it interfere with daily life though, and still shopped, explored, and met locals with minimum fuss – for a few days. However, my resolve to continue unflustered didn't last; I soon succumbed. To bed it was.

After a while I had a particularly sensitive problem. In straight talking terms, I was out of clean underwear. I knew of a local market which stocked everything under the sun and set about a plan: to rush to the market, buy what I needed to stock up on in order to survive in my hotel room, and sprint back, all between the required (and getting ever-shorter) bathroom breaks.

Well, in sum, it worked; success! I had a new supply of underwear for the long road ahead. On reflection though, how peculiar the sight must have been, for a Russian market trader seeing a bewildered tourist running around at light-speed, at once the desperation and determination prominent on his face, buying random clothing articles before sprinting out of the market and back up the street as fast as he could go.

The city, unlike many in this region, had never been closed to foreigners in the past. I wondered whether the polished exterior and pleasant lifestyle enjoyed here in the summer and autumn came from the lack of cultural isolation that many Siberian cities seemed to possess. Was it the apparent influences from Europe, the ornate architecture and enjoyable secluded lifestyle being unsurpassed in Siberia? Maybe I had just experienced plain and simple good luck, to be here whilst the sun was shining at its brightest.

Far from being a merely pleasant, largely undiscovered rural city though, Khabarovsk lays claim to several cultural points of importance. The local university, The Pacific National University used to be a polytechnic but now enjoys full university status. Dynamo Park, which has a strip stretching up from the beach north east to the Park proper, a few blocks from the Promenade, is also a delight. To the south of the park are water pools and picnic areas, accompanied by local teenagers rollerblading past pensioners eating their sandwiches in the early afternoon sun. Follow Sheronova Street south east and you'll come across the city's vast and colourful arboretum, which dates from 1896 when it was used as an experimental horticultural lab.

Anyway, back to the hydrofoil.

Heading away from Khabarovsk, the blue waters ebbed and drifted by the cold steely grey of the boat's hull. We had said our friendly goodbyes to Lina and Valeriya a few nights before, the excitement of prospective 'holiday romance' petering out after a few more vodka fueled but ultimately duller meetings. We drank, saw the sights, chatted through the evenings, but it was to go no further. They had their lives to live, and sadly we were leaving.

Craig and I had taken a very early morning taxi to the dock to catch the boat. Craig was indefatigably interested in the boat's engineering and the river's course, but I was silent. I tried to get some more sleep – it was a state in which I wouldn't succumb to the stomach virus. We set off around 6.00 am from Kharbarovsk, and the hydrofoil was expected to take nearly seven hours to reach its destination. The journey drifted by slowly. Just after midday, with the sun beating down on us, the boat slowed a gear and spun a 180 degree turn in the river channel. It did so in order to moor on the west bank to our left. I lurched from my sleep with a bump – we had finally arrived at Komsomolsk-na-Amure.

The city sits on the west bank of the river and has repute as the site of many machine building and timber companies. It has, as have many cities in this region, a rich history of foundation and rose with the Mongol empire, followed by Soviet domination in the mid-19th century. Although it is far from European Russia, far-flung provincial cities with blue collar economies like this seem to be doing well, and the detailed Stalinist architecture gave an almost romantic, prosperous frontier-like atmosphere to the place. The 'Wild East', perhaps? Whilst we were visiting in the fair autumnal climate, in January it would get as low as -30 degrees Celsius.

As soon as we had departed the boat, the sooner no-one was in site. This was not a harbour, merely a mooring point from which we had disembarked, nothing more. I looked back and even the boat had left.

As Craig and I looked around, the direction the town lay in was clear; there weren't many other directions to go in. The War Memorial, a substantial structure of seven granite heads all looking at an eternal flame, towered above the river terminal. We sauntered up Mira Prospekt, or Peace Street, before finding a cafe which served minuscule portions of *pelmeni*. I ordered two portions, and another milky tea, from a wiry waitress with a sour demeanour. The wooden stairs that led up to the cafe creaked as another patron entered. The place was decorated as to be bohemian – red wallpaper, funky art, and photos of crazy places and crazier people. But to me, in my ill and irritable state, it lacked something. I guess it may have been charming in its own ironic, lacklustre way.

I stood in a pharmacy in a small rural city, about as far from anywhere as you could be, about to try and order diarrhea relief in my half-baked Russian, conscious that this would be quite embarrassing in the least. I had no idea what was coming.

For a start, my attempts at Russian fell on deaf ears, and the pharmacist either wouldn't or couldn't understand me. Craig stepped in, but even with his command of the language the pharmacist was not playing ball.

The pharmacist was a rather rotund woman with cropped strawberry blonde hair. Her glasses framed a slightly flushed and annoyed face; a face hinting at dissatisfaction with her job perhaps? The awkwardness between us did not subside, so our measures had to get rather more practical. What had started as an innocent attempt to resolve my problem – going strong for over two weeks now – had therefore descended into my best friend now publicly miming having the runs, performance complete with sounds and facial contortions; whilst performing a hand gesture which involved splaying his hand dramatically downwards out of the direction of his behind, in an attempt to secure me a remedy. The curious thing was, a similar incident had occurred when Craig tried to buy some toilet paper in Beijing – the transaction again descended into miming the act of going to the toilet with a lot of effort going into Craig's character acting, much to the amusement of the cashier. Regaling this tale later, another backpacker told me that there is in fact a much more civilised and internationally accepted sign to do with your hands if you need to secure some toilet paper; moving your index fingers around each other in a circle (mimicking the shape of the toilet roll). So simple. So amazing neither of us thought of it.

Still, Craig was an invaluable ally – and crucially, the pharmacist now handed over the drug we were ordering, albeit with a smile.

Compared with the subdued beauty of Khabarovsk, Komsomolsk seemed much more unrefined. Visible from the outset was the fact that this really wasn't a priority sight-seeing location. Gone were Khabarovsk's dreaming spires and leafy boulevards, in place was a real Soviet era throwback, concrete tower blocks and crumbling road edges. The city's Stalinist renaissance architecture softened the edges a little, and it had a river beach like Khabarovsk's, although much smaller. There was also an abundance of patriotic painted murals on the city's walls, excellent for an amateur photographer like me, giving a dash of intense colour to an otherwise drab area.

I lay in the hotel and thought of the eastbound Russian explorers of the 18th and 19th centuries, pushing into Siberia for their country, fighting skirmishes over towns like this with the Chinese pushing north from Manchuria and the Koreans who laid claim too. Here though my thoughts were off the mark, as this town had never been part of that. Although a railway town by pedigree and now home to major industry (similar to Khabarovsk), Komsomolsk harbours a different type of disturbing past; being one of the major *gulag* centres (concentration camps) which used many German and Japanese POWs to complete work on the Baikal-Amur Mainline railway, as many as 150,000 people dying in the process. Rising to prominence in the 1930s, the locals would like to think that Komsomolsk is a shining example of patriotism, of founding a city against the odds and completing the major railway line in the region, of glory and honour. But in truth, Komsomolsk-na-Amure's history ought to be a less celebratory affair.

Having now seen the Far East of Russia, our thoughts returned to travelling westward. To get to Central Asia through Russia, we would have to go via Lake Baikal. Unequivocally synonymous with Siberia, Baikal is the largest freshwater lake in the world and the source of one-fifth of the world's freshwater supply.

Our plan was to use the Baikal-Amur Mainline (or BAM) which runs fairly parallel to the Trans-Siberian line but a couple of hundred miles further north, to get to the northern tip of Lake Baikal, at a town called Severobaikalsk. To do so, we had to board a train bound for Tynda, a principal city of Siberia, and one of the furthest places north we could expect to encounter. However, on arriving at Komsomolsk station, we discovered that there was nothing bound for Tynda for most of the rest of the week, so in order to keep moving we resigned ourselves to getting aboard an earlier train headed for Skovorodino, a small rural town where the railway forked. We would change trains, and head to the southern tip of Baikal instead; and from there on to Novosibirsk.

The BAM was initially built for military purposes, as a back-up for the Trans-Siberian which runs too close to the Chinese border for long sections. The construction project, like most enduring labours, suffered its fair share of setbacks. As well as claiming the lives of thousands of prisoners of war, work ceased on the line as a result of Stalin's death. Resuming in 1974, using no prisoners – 'clean hands only' – to continue the build, it was officially finished in 1984, although construction did continue until as late as 1991.The line offers quite a different journey to the Trans-Siberian, some of the travellers using it opting to leave at the biggest station, Komsomolsk, but others pushing forward to the Pacific edge and onward to Sakhalin Island, a large, long and thin island off Russia's Pacific coast, owned by Russia but which has been firmly in territorial dispute with Japan in the past. Sakhalin still runs a few ferry options to Japan.

Curiously, the various nationalities of gulag prisoners who built the Baikal-Amur Mainline left their own influence by imposing their architectural and cultural flair on the stations they built as they progressed down the line. Each station is unique and has its own feel to it; passing through each is its own experience, and you could travel only the BAM and still learn more about the *gulag* and the train line than read in any book. I had heard that the Ukrainian and Kazakhstani stations were not to be missed, and the station at Severobaikalsk was turned out in a splendid Leningrad style.

We got tickets for our revised route – through more of my pidgin Russian – and boarded the train yet again, clambering up the ladder direct from the gravel rather than from the platform. Yes, it was not the original plan, but we had to keep moving. We were on route to Central Asia, via Skovorodino.

On the train rides we had experienced so far, both Craig and I had become the subject of many people's inquisitiveness, attracting questions and prolonged looks from the locals also travelling by rail. The travellers were mostly male. I had noticed a particular style of haircut amongst the Russian men, whereby they all seemed to have had the backs and sides shaved short, but then combed the top of their hair forward down their foreheads. They often had gel to keep it in place. I guess it was some sort of masculine thing, a look native to the working-class poverty and violence prevalent in many parts of Russia. The men's vests, gold teeth, and tracksuits complemented the look; minor gangsters in small towns, the type of places where anything goes.

On one occasion I was sat around the fold-down table which sat between the bunk beds, four or six of us sat on the lower bunk which became our bench for the table. We would talk and drink, and it was mostly because we weren't from around their parts that they wanted to talk.

The local guys were trying it on a bit with a scam, asking us to produce one dollar, which they would write their address on, or some such other message. They insisted many times that they didn't want the dollar for themselves, only for us to have a souvenir of having met them. Something didn't sit right; Craig and I suspected that they wanted to see where we kept our wallets in order to have a rummage later, or to gauge our wealth for a future scam. So we politely declined their offer. This seemed to cause offence within the group, who were becomingly increasingly drunk. We had all had a couple of beers, but I wasn't that drunk. One guy, after having his persistence refused for the last time, got angry and aggressive with me, raising his voice and becoming violent. He was sat on the opposite corner to me so wasn't a direct threat, but he did pick up a beer can and throw it at me, hitting me square in the forehead. At this point things got a little more sober, with me angrily repeating the only phrase I could remember in Russian after drinking and being confronted with this guy.

"*Nyet kharasho*" I stressed – literally meaning 'no good' in English.

I was trying to say that that was 'not cool', and frankly I was embarrassed because my Russian was usually better than that – but I think the message was heard. One of the other locals, an elder charismatic guy, apologised on the aggressor's behalf.

"Ignore him", he insisted.

"You oughtta calm down", he continued to press on the drunkard, who was increasingly being nudged by his mates who all looked a bit shocked.

Whilst apologising, he made it clear he didn't want foreigners to think his own people were all like this; unreasonable and surly. At this point my thoughts wandered. I had witnessed one random act of aggression from a guy who probably really couldn't compute what Craig and I were doing here, and almost instantly after an act of compassion, kindness, and reason which instantly negated the former. I think for the first time I began to realise thoughts which have stayed with me to this day; that people the world over are essentially the same. The only difference between them is that they are kept apart by differing politics, traditions, and potentially our egos, our own greed. The Siberian arsehole sat in front of me being forced to apologise through gritted teeth was the same as the deprived taxi drivers in Beijing and the gangsters in the Mongolian nightclub. The elder Samaritan mediating this brawl could equally be the Chinese student pleading the case on our behalf to the greedy taxi drivers back in China. Languages, education, geography; all of these things fluctuate, but I think human society will always have this innate moral balance.

Arriving at Skovorodino, the summer I had endured in China, left behind in Mongolia, and briefly rediscovered in Russia's Far East was dissipating again; this time for good. The trees were now a richer shade of auburn, the curl of the burnt brown leaves a stark reminder of autumn, and the depression in the air was distinctly chillier than any I'd yet to be familiar with.

The town sat low on the landscape, and to my left I could see a climbing hill covered in evergreen forest. Long-established ways of living were clear. Farms and corrugated iron outbuildings dotted the backdrop, and a smoking chimney broke through the canopy of the woodland, the grey haze drifting upward against a rich blue autumn sky. Everywhere there was a pleasing silence, punctuated only by birds' occasional twitter.

I wandered from the station up into the town, where there appeared to be little indications of life. I passed a small, simple news agents store. The dirty glass windows obscured the view inside, and the white paint was peeling from the wooden door frame. Here, like everywhere else, simple cafes and bare shop shelves represented life in provincial Russia. There was another of the striking Orthodox churches in town too, a beacon made of sterile brickwork. Here, Orthodox religion casts its watchful eye over an otherwise colourless and down-at-heel stopover. There was no other person on the streets here – I seem to remember the inside of the church was just as quiet as the outside.

The guide books on Siberia may not mention much about the town of Skovorodino, for ample reason. It is tiny, and we didn't encounter anybody or any place worth reciting here. The town may soon be revived though, as an oil pipeline is being built from Tayshet, which is north west over the other side of Lake Baikal, down to Skovorodino and continuing on by rail. The idea is to make onward oil to China and the east a more viable option.

Our stay here was limited, as we had to push on forward to the lake. Our onward train didn't depart until around 5.00 am the following morning, and with no accommodation available in the town, it looked like I would be spending a night sleeping at a station in Russia. There were a few sinister-looking guys around, so we took it in turns to doze as best we could on the plastic seats, and kept our bags tied to us. The station itself was dingy and looked seldom cleaned; there were staff I noticed occasionally, but no-one on the kiosk and their presence was certainly lacking. The dim, florescent light which hung loosely from the ceiling flickered, adding to the sense of deprivation. Occasionally some locals would come over and make polite conversation; others avoided us like the plague. A middle-aged mother with her teenage son were waiting for the same train as us, a small comfort that we had other passengers travelling the same way as us. I added another layer or two; but by around 2.00 am I was really feeling the bitterness of the cold.

An unkempt and shady man accompanied by a rough unpleasant woman came through the station's entrance staggering, possibly drunk or worse, offering to sell *kartochki*; pre-paid phone cards. I suspected it was a scam, perhaps the cards were used up, or maybe they just wanted to see where you kept your wallet in order to nab it later. Either way, I made little eye contact and heeded their movements. The woman, with greasy dark blonde hair and crooked teeth, looked disheveled, her tattered clothes hanging from her undernourished body. The man, who I assumed was her partner, wore similarly tattered clothes, a track suit with battered trainers, and his face was unshaven and gaunt. His black hair was thinning and was greased back over his skull. The pair stood there, expectant. The female offered the statement to the whole station lobby:

"*Kartochki* for sale! ..." before roaming around the place to see if anyone was interested.

The Russian people are a folk who have sacrifice running thick through their blood. Hardship is not new to them. This pair were no different.

Condensation formed in the air from the woman's breath. As she stood there, anxious and flitting, she repeated her request to me.

Almost shouting, she demanded in Russian: "Well, do you wanna buy the *kartochki*?" before proceeding to rummage into a sports bag.

I replied in the negative, to which the pair paused to look at me for longer than a moment. With an air of sulkiness, they drifted off again onto the platform.

Finally, the train arrived, a vast leviathan of metal groaning to a halt amid the frosted and slippy concrete of the platform. I threw my rucksack aboard ahead of me, and clambered up the ladder, stiff from the chill. It was nearly dawn, but I for one welcomed sleep.

As the train pressed on, throughout the next day, I met my

fellow passengers. In the same compartment as Craig and I were two middle-aged women, a little too young to be *babushkas* but still of that style; wearing simple skirts and woolen pull-overs, completing the look with head-over shawls and thick scratchy looking blankets. They liked their tea black, and sickly sweet.

"Chai?", they offered, with a smile.

They even had a jar of honey with them, a more convenient and in my opinion a tastier alternative to sugar. They were warm and mothering, offering us extra blankets and making us cups of tea if they went to the samovar. They shared some doughy bread with us at one lunch time too. I had picked up a cold, and they insisted on plying me with tea and honey throughout our time together. Tea and honey will cure almost anything in the eyes of Russian housewives.

Towards the front of the carriage was a group of Russian males, getting drunk, but thankfully not aggressive. They invited us to drink with them, but we were initially cautious. It was rude to decline, and we wanted to have fun with the locals. Craig and I sat down with them. They had vodka, as well as brandy, other spirits and beer. They could sense that we were a little apprehensive but that all changed once the guys introduced themselves.

"I'm the Chief of police around here", said one, almost immediately.

His words hung in the air as Craig and I turned to look at each other with a small smile.

He showed us his detective's ID card proudly, like someone would with a picture of their kids from a wallet, this ID kept crisp and safe in his inside jacket pocket. It was in Cyrillic, obviously, so it could have been a blockbuster video card for all I knew. Fulfilling the stereotype, he was overweight, wore a black leather jacket and a grey Cossack hat, and had a three-day stubble growth.

"They all work for me", he indicated, not looking, but waving his finger behind him in the general direction of the others – it hovering toward them for a little longer than was necessary.

We lightened up a little and joined in the drinking. The night was growing colder, and the train's heaters seemed to not be on. I had seven layers on; all the clothing I owned.

The conversation flowed and I gradually began to feel warmer, it was probably the alcohol. The police Chief set a fine moral example, and a few hours of laughter, risqué banter, and spilt drinks later he was slumped forward on his table, barely conscious. He occasionally tried to come to, but his efforts were thwarted by the alcohol. He vomited on himself and the slobber slimed down his chin and onto the plastic table top. His gang of subordinates found it all immensely funny, as did I at the time. They howled with laughter, propping the Chief up on his own elbows, or prodding him back to consciousness from time to time.

As usual, the guys were mildly interested in where we were from, but the rowdy banter soon descended into talk of things which were the talk of all men the world over; family, jobs, and girls. Soon, the session was drawing to a close, so I clambered up to the top bunk in my compartment, having to stand on the middle-aged women's bunks in order to do so. Drunk, I imagine I made quite a racket, grabbing the top bunks and heaving my legs up onto the higher mattress. I still felt cold, yet managed to fall asleep almost immediately, still wearing all my layers.

Later on this section of the railway, the party of policemen got off the train. The morning after the drinking, they got up, politely saying their goodbyes, all smiles and handshakes, and departed the train. They weren't at all embarrassed about the night before, and I got the impression that they expected that behaviour to be considered normal, despite being police officers. I suppose they were off duty after all.

The remainder of the journey passed without major incident. It was a pleasant couple of days on board, the train an older one than I'd yet travelled, complete with wooden paneling and a much simpler toilet which was really just a hole in the metal floor. Arriving into the same carriage as me the day afterwards was a young lad, roughly 17 years old, who spoke a little heavily-accented English and was happy to talk. He had an inquisitive nature and a western perspective to his opinions. Well turned out, he wore a simple white polo shirt and had neat side-parted brown hair, and a gaunt face.

He was also headed west, to his University in Moscow.

"I study music", he said. "I play the cello".

We talked further about his studies and Russia. Before long, we were talking about Russian culture and what I had experienced on my trip so far.

"I don't understand the Russian way, to get drunk all the time" he observed; "it's not necessary".

It was clear that his middle-class background and education separated him from the likes of the policemen, those born into poverty and living for the next meal, the next *sto gram* of vodka. But at the same time, I was glad. His obvious dislike of such behaviour set him apart from the norms of this region. He seemed to have a bright future ahead of him with his studies in the city.

This boy listened intently as I spoke of my travels so far, occasionally his forehead wrinkling with surprise as he wondered about these other sites of the world he was yet to experience. After hearing of the journey, and my relative ease at crossing the borders, he bantered that I was a British spy – how else could I travel so easily and speak Russian to the locals in such a manner?

We played cards and continued to talk; of everything and of nothing. Craig's bunk was located two carriages down and was near the bunk of the young lad's mother. This meant that for a change I got to know people in my carriage using my level of Russian, by not having Craig's expertise and prior cultural knowledge to rely on, taking me beyond my comfort zone. It was a good feeling.

I guess time is relative, but it didn't seem to take long before the railway saddled up parallel to the great Lake Baikal. For kilometres the tracks meander beside the shore, and travelling from east to west the lake was out the right hand side of the train. The grey rocks and pebbles which lined the lake's shore gave way to dust and grass just inches from the railway line. The trees lined the lake shore, some still bright green, and slightly swaying in the wind. As your eyes drifted west to the other side of the lake it was a different scene altogether, the pebbly beach underfoot on this side contrasted by large cliffs plunging cleanly into the water on the other. It was a bright morning, and early, and in the autumn air the waters looked crisp and immaculate; unbroken and spanning endlessly north.

Craig and I walked along the shore of Baikal, flicking smooth stones in to the lake, skimming them across the surface. Most of the beach was full of grey and dark pebbles, turning into grass further up, which in turn led to areas of trees along the lake's edge in places. Where I was now, on the southern shore, the land was flat and pebbly. To the west, the shore's cliffs gave way to hills. Look northwards, and the lake was more of a sea. Land on the horizon wasn't visible at all. The opposite side of the shore was clearly visible that morning, as the sky was a bright shade of light blue. The surrounding land of the eastern shore was seemingly untouched. Looking at a map, there are towns dotted around the lake, but the sheer size of the body of water meant that there were entire stretches of untouched coastline visible, where the rolling mounds plunged deep under the water line. In the summer, many come here for the water sports such as boating and for free-diving, a sport where you dive completely unaided, without oxygen tanks. In the winter much of the lake is frozen and vehicles suitable for such tasks make the journey to and from shore-side towns opposite sides of the thick frozen ice.

The town of Sludyanka sits on the southerly tip of Lake Baikal and is a popular point for tourists to experience the lake in season. This time of year there were no other foreigners around, and we made our way to a local Orthodox church to kill some time. We could see it as we made our way from the railway tracks down to the pebbly southern shore of Baikal. It stood dejected and barely used, just a couple of hundred metres away from the water. Clouds had been gathering more and more since we had been travelling west, and today the cross which stood atop the church tower sat against a grey and menacing sky. The grey of the bricks and the dark maroon of the rusty iron fencing which barely remained gave the air of a creepy building which would fit quite neatly into the set of a low budget zombie movie. Moss grew up the walls, and the aged door looked barely used. From reading a sign outside in my poor Russian it was clear that services were still held there regularly enough. A tattered graveyard sticking out on the east side of the church only added to the atmosphere of desperation. The battered and angled tombstones sat amongst clumps of grass and shrubs which had not been tended to in some time. A cast iron fence ringed the lot, again, bent out of shape and rusting with age.

Wandering south, away from the lake and the church and across the railway line, lay the main component of the town. There was a central square with a bus station in the centre with a few newspaper and confectionery vendors, but nothing else out of the ordinary. Around the edges of the square were a few average-looking cafes, newsagents, and similar shops. Craig and I entered a cafe across the road and took a look at the menu. It looked good, full of Russian hearty meals, with my favourite *borshch* and the ubiquitous *beefsteaks* and the like. However, they only had a few things left in the kitchen, like most cafes in Russia, and some soup and fries with some own-brand Coca-Cola would have to satisfy us.

The girl behind the counter was attractive, blonde, but like most Russians not so easy to read. She hadn't met foreigners who could speak Russian before, at least not that many that I could discern, and I think we appeared something strange. She was young, a teenager, but at the same time seemed old beyond her years. As we talked, it was apparent she didn't want to be in Sludyanka, a town that was a backwater and really only a source of income from the tourists, Russian and international, that stopped here as a by-product of coming to visit the lake.

"There's not loads for a teenager growing up here to do. I'm bored..." she shared, wistfully, staring out through the doorway, leaning her elbows on the counter.

And like that, with a "ho hum", she snapped out of it, turned and walked out back, out of sight behind the counter.

Craig had managed to find out that across town there was a *banya*, a Russian sauna house, so we went over to the (very hard to find) address and enquired. The building seemed a typical house as far as I could tell. After even finding the right street, we had a bit of trouble working out if it even was a *banya* and whether it was actually open for business or not. There were grimy windows and a weathered feel to it, with a sad looking tree growing out of the front yard area, which was mostly mud and soil anyway. Craig had been wanting a *banya* for a long time, he said it was the perfect way to unwind. Not only that, but the bathroom on the train was lacking and we hadn't showered. Some of the Russians had taught me ways to shower in the train, from rigging a pre-bought, pre-cut length of hose pipe to the tap in the sink, to using a 2-litre bottle with holes punctured in it, filled with water, to hang above your head. Others advocated the frugal face and pits wash only, for the duration of the journey. However, all of these options weren't great, and besides, a *banya* managed to clear your pores like nothing else.

"Shall we go in?" I ventured.

We did enter and it was deserted. A wooden desk and dark walls were all that were to be seen. We looked around a bit, and eventually came across a female with a stocky frame and a red beehive hairdo. She told us that the male *banya* was unfortunately closed today. For females it was open, but they alternated the sexes through the days of the week.

"Would you return tomorrow?" she offered, politely.

We could not.

The next part of the journey into Novosibirsk passed well. The belligerence and wary attitude towards travellers by the Siberian people Craig and I had met was gradually replaced by complacency and eventually, the odd amiable introduction from those we met.

By now I was used to the long haul train rides, the thump of the carriage over the railway sleepers, and the ever changing views from the window which seemed to morph effortlessly from the steppe of stubbly grass, to lusher more forested areas into rural settlements, and then cycle back again, all while occasionally receiving a light dusting of snow. Most of the time I would read a book or listen to music on my Japanese mp3 player to pass the time. I tended to sleep intermittently for a few hours at a time, both as a result of having to be in a bunk for the whole journey, but also for other reasons of security. I could never sleep totally soundly whilst a stranger was in close proximity to all of my worldly belongings. Both mine and Craig's rucksacks were locked and stowed in a compartment underneath the lower bunk bed, and we were up in the top bunk for the parts of the journey where we weren't sat around drinking tea, playing cards, or attempting to have a conversation in Russian. The compartment was accessed by lifting up the lower bunk's mattress, and then a plyboard on a hinge to reveal the cubby hole below. So, when we were asleep our luggage could possibly be accessed by those below us – or worse, if we made a stop and the passenger below got off the train in the middle of the night, the compartment was left totally unguarded for those on the carriage (or anybody who subsequently alighted) to potentially access.

However, the journey passed well, and all my property remained intact. The train arrived exactly on time into Novosibirsk station. I said goodbye to the gaunt musician who was still with us, making his way back to Moscow.

"Good luck" he wished me.

I smiled back, and genuinely wished him luck with everything in return.

I swung open the train door and both Craig and I stepped down onto the platform. It was early, perhaps 7.00 am, but I for one felt refreshed and ready to explore the self-proclaimed capital of Siberia. The station was not like any I'd seen in Russia yet; it was larger for a start, and there were many other commuters, posters, and vending machines. A proper urban hub. As we geographically moved west, it followed that we moved further towards western capitalism.

With the ambling crowds I made my way through some dark corridors through to the main station reception, a large area which seemed richly decorated with supple carpets and marble.

Stepping outside it was clear that the station's interior matched the exterior. It was a suitably grand building which dominated the central city area. The building was a refreshing bright shade of mint green, with bold white edging, corners, and window frames. There was a large, open square in front of the station which was used by traders, newsagents, and taxi ranks, the relative emptiness of which contrasted against the 'busy-ness' of the station building and its tall, bold authority, demanding your eye is drawn back to it.

Most of the time whilst travelling we would book a relatively cheap hostel or hotel for a night or two, before using those 24 or 48 hours of flexibility to find somewhere cheaper, nicer, or more recommended by the locals. In Novosibirsk though, there weren't many hostels to choose from – only hotels – and even then, they weren't of the type we could really spend money on. They were either expensive, or not convenient.

Craig and I began to explore the city by foot, going to the addresses of listed hostels to find out if they could take us; but it never even got that far, as weirdly none we chose appeared to be open. Instead, we resorted to trying to find an internet cafe to further our search. We had a guide book for the area on us and used it to look up an internet cafe to visit. We had all day, so we weren't too worried about it. I had already slept in a railway station recently and had no apprehension about roughing it for a bit.

Our morning had been used up from trekking all over, but an hour or two searching for guesthouses or unused university halls on the internet might prove successful. There were two listed in the guide, and the one which was nearest was a few blocks away. I think it took us about 20 minutes to get to the address, which didn't contain any thing even resembling an internet cafe. The nearest address was a school and thinking there may be a communal internet cafe for use on the premises, we took a look round.

Entering a school armed only with the excuse that I was looking for an internet terminal is not something I would dare to consider in Britain, but here we had little other options. It turned out to be deserted for some reason, but that meant that a lot of the doors were locked. We wandered through empty tarmac areas. The main bulk of the school was three storeys high, and fairly uninspiring, like any comprehensive school anywhere. The rear playground and sports fields led to another street, so we perused there for any sign of a cafe but found none. For some reason both Craig and I were determined that the net cafe would be here.

We reasoned with ourselves, our inner voice trying to square the circle. There weren't many internet resources around here, so surely a school would make a perfect spot to combine net access?

We re-entered the property and wandered through the corridors. We came to a stairwell which led down to a basement, but those doors were locked too. We had to bite the bullet; our ridiculous and possibly illegal search of a school for an internet cafe had to end. Not before we decided to leave, cue stage right, a rather worried looking teacher appeared, complete with security guards to escort us from the premises. I think we were very lucky indeed.

There was another one the other side of town, which charged a little more per hour but was used mainly for internet gamers. This was good – it meant higher bandwidth and speedier internet access. The place was a real geek's heaven, computer games and posters everywhere. An emo-style brunette girl served us at the counter. She had a quite serious demeanour like a lot of Russian people; she looked like she might be a challenge to break the ice with.

We sat down and logged on. I had heard of a website called couchsurfing which was essentially a goodwill gesture for travellers everywhere. The concept was that every traveller could search online for hospitality and reciprocate where possible. I loved that travellers from all over could experience someone else's life and gain new perspectives on things. On the website, you searched through any logical search terms; location, duration of offered (or proposed) stay, gender of host and so on. I was keen to give it a try, but Craig was less so. He rightly thought we could get into some unwanted trouble, and that quite frankly it was a little weird. In these circumstances though, we had to at least try it. As it turned out, after I'd emailed a few people, a couple called Semen and Valentina got back in touch. It was in the nick of time; they really did us a very kind gesture by offering us a bed for a couple of nights and the promise of a decent meal. After getting directions to their place we set off. We had to take a little city minibus out into the suburbs, but we didn't care. It was off the beaten track and it was a warm flat to go to.

The minibus ground its gears and revved its way through the slushy autumnal streets. The city was overcast, and it had started to rain. The other traffic was made up of equally aged vehicles, Ladas and Skodas everywhere, with the odd classic old Mercedes saloon. For the first time since being in Japan I remember hearing a radio station playing western pop music in the vehicle. Inside, the minibus was full up and we were crammed in near the back next to a lot of other people's luggage. We crossed a large bridge and turned off the main road. The rain eased off slightly as the streets gradually got narrower, more neglected, and less crowded. The visibility in the rainy traffic was still not very good though, although you could just about make out other headlights in the downpour. After about 45 minutes Craig and I arrived at our stop and found ourselves like so many other times on this trip, stood on a crumbling kerb in the middle of nowhere, squinting at a map.

Semen and Valentina opened the door to their apartment and welcomed us in. There was a small utility room where we could leave our trainers and rucksacks before going into the main corridor from where the other rooms were accessed. Turning right from the corridor took you into their kitchen, turning left into their bedroom. Further right from the kitchen was the bathroom door, and further left still took you to a separate room where one of their grandparents lived, choosing to remain as separate as possible. We gathered this may because of his dislike of foreigners, and therefore our mere presence, although we never found out for sure. We could sleep on the floor of their bedroom.

"Would that be OK?"

To us, it was the Hilton.

Their kitchen was small, white and fairly modern. There was a small spread of food on their table; some cakes, tea, and fruit, all delicately presented on a pristine white tablecloth. Here was a couple who had very little, but enjoyed hosting and learning about travellers, and whose generosity overwhelmed me.

Valentina had long brown hair which sat contently just below her shoulders. Her eyes were sharp and inquisitive. Her laid-back smile betrayed confidence and she made us feel at home.

"*Dobray veecher*" - 'good evening', she said kindly.

"*Privyet... kak deela?*"

As a university student she was more than capable of a sustained conversation with us in English, and we quickly switched to that.

Talk turned to subjects such as "how do you find Novosibirsk", "how is the weather for you" and such. The pleasantries were warm and genuine, and the ice didn't take long to break, if at all. The cakes were homemade and delicious – and I took great pleasure in reminding them of it.

The 'Lord of the East'

Vladivostok, home to Russia's Eastern fleet

Back in the USSR

Shashlik Beach

Russian architecture

Looking back towards Vladivostok station

Symmetry, near Skovorodino, I believe

Artwork in Komsomolsk

The church in Khabarovsk

Walking the shores of Lake Baikal

Sludyanka

Novosibirsk smoulders

Novosibirsk station

Almaty from the hills

Almaty sunset

Medeo Stadium, near Almaty

Buildings surrounding Medeo

Urban neglect

Almaty, with the 'fastcoaster' in the foreground

A mosque in Aktobe

'Russia has a future. Terrorism does not'

Panfilov Park, Almaty

Moscow river views

Red Square

'Lenin'

The famous St Basil's Cathedral

Semen was handsome, stocky, and blond; he reminded me of a rugby player. He stood back a little, happy to follow Valentina's lead.

She had offered us a seat and we sat around their small table. The talk soon became chat, and the chat soon became sharing. It was a lovely evening. We chatted about lots of things. Valentina was interested in our trip and where we were going next; as it happened, they had both been on holiday to Central Asia before and showed us some photos of their trip into Kazakhstan and Kyrgyzstan. They had a close call at a currency exchange booth where they were nearly ripped off. Semen appeared less willing to talk, but it soon became clear that his reticence was because he wasn't very comfortable with his level of English. The gaps in conversation were filled with a slight peppering of Russian, an explanatory word here and there. We continued to talk, the conversation shifting to what there was to really experience here in Novosibirsk. Nearby there was a large market worth checking out, and nearer the centre there were a few decent restaurants. As we explained to them, we weren't massively keen on being touristy but instead wanted to soak up the atmosphere of the places we visited. For this we could have done a lot worse than wandering the city and getting the lowdown from Semen and Valentina.

Novosibirsk sits on the Ob River, a major waterway which runs from the Altai Mountains positioned to the south of the city, zigzagging back and forth all the way north until its mouth widens into the Arctic Circle. The Altais lie across the four-way border between Russia, China, Mongolia, and Kazakhstan, right in the middle of Asia. Literally meaning 'Mountains of Gold', the steep peaks rise to their highest in the north west where the mountains are particularly unforgiving. The navigable passes are few and far between, and from there the range extends south-east where it gradually turns into a plateau and subsequently into what is the Gobi Desert of Mongolia. The region is home to both the snow leopard and the rare Siberian ibex and is a World Heritage Site. Heading north from Novosibirsk, the river's course tumbles and turns through the steppe, tundra, and marshes typical of Siberia. Further still, it has the longest river estuary in the world, which eventually flows into the 600-mile-long Gulf of Ob, and on then into the Kara Sea, which is in turn part of the Arctic Ocean.

The city itself was founded back in 1893 when the Trans-Siberian railway engineers identified the need for the railway to cross the river at that point. Named Novonikolayevsk after Tsar Nicholas II, it was renamed Novosibirsk in 1926, the new mantle literally meaning 'New Siberian City'. Now it is the third largest city in Russia, after Moscow and St. Petersburg, and is Siberia's largest city and administrative capital. The winters are like most in Russia, perilously cold, with temperatures reaching -40 degrees Celsius. The summers are milder and reasonably hot by comparison. Like many railway-founded towns, it has industrial roots, and this was clear from the sight of factories and hazy smoke stacks lining the flanks of the river as it flows north, all visible through the fog from the window of Valentina and Semen's flat.

The tower block which my hosts resided in reminded me of the eyesores in Mongolia; communal blocks which are throwbacks to the Soviets and are now commonly disused, dourly tolerated or disguised with fresh paint. Their block was one of a few which faced onto a communal playground area, with some patchy grass, some concrete, and some tables which had seen better days. Oddly there was a battered old table tennis table set up outside and we had a little knock-about.

"Am I being hussled?!" I joked, as Valentina won a game – again.

Despite the presence of the other tower blocks, hardly anybody else passed us by as we walked and talked throughout the lonely and murky area. We had been warned about being out here at night, and it was clear why. Later, viewing the area from the security of the flat in the evening, the concrete, which was weathered and yielding to the harsh northern elements was illuminated only sporadically by pools of dim light from solitary lamp posts, none of which offered much security, or would even be that beneficial in highlighting a crime to a potential passing rescuer. Some indeterminable distance away, a dog barked repeatedly.

Other than the barking, the nights here in the suburbs seemed to hold only pitiless silence.

Downtown Novosibirsk was really very pleasant. The city had plenty of cafes, shops, and conveniences. It's also home to a university of some repute and as such the city has heaps of young people. One convenience not to my taste was the sole sushi restaurant, which isn't too far from the central square. Growing up I was taught to be wary of eating fish if you weren't near the sea – and unfortunately for this place, Novosibirsk is pretty much as far inland as you can get in the world. As usual, there sits the token statue of Lenin in the city centre, on this occasion surrounded by a fine, well-tended square.

Whilst walking around, I passed a massive mural of graffiti, which was pro-state advertising. It was a colourful picture of some rebels being quashed by upstanding Russian military or FSB operatives dressed in camouflage and black police gear. The whole thing stood probably ten feet tall, along about 30 feet stretch of board being used on the side of a building. It was a work of art but had been there long enough to accumulate glued-on posters and flyers for music events and shop sales, obscuring the mural a bit, although even these were fraying at the edges.

One section of the mural had an FSB agent cradling a young vulnerable child whilst warding off rebels. Underneath in Cyrillic was written a rather righteous message, portraying the potential of this vast country.

It put its case simply and straightforwardly: "Russia has a future; terrorism does not".

By this time both Craig and I had seen a lot of the city and we had been hosted so amazingly by Semen and Valentina. They were so polite and had often been insinuating that it was they who should be thankful. For the price of sharing a few small meals, they had managed to practise their English, hear some stories of foreign lands, and help out these two wayward strays in need. So, when we came to leave the city, overwhelmed by our hosts' welcome and undivided hospitality, I felt moved. We had spent far too short a time here. I would be visiting Russia again on this trip, but for now my time in Siberia was drawing to a close. I was excited to be heading to Kazakhstan, but I knew it would be hard to experience the times I'd had in Russia again.

As a parting shot, I'd have to do a little Russian language test – I'd have to order the train tickets in Russian again. This time no help, correct sentences, no pieces of English here and there. Just do it.

Back in the railway station, I approached the booth and began to order the tickets. I'd rehearsed the ticket requirements and the teller seemed satisfied with the details I supplied. She asked me a question in Russian which I needed her to repeat, but essentially we were there.

The train left tomorrow, and thanks to me we were booked on it.

The Russian trains I had favoured using on this trip had so far been clean, reasonably comfortable, and not over-crowded. When buying the tickets into Kazakhstan, Craig and I always made a point of asking which nation the train was from, in order to gauge the level of reliability and comfort of the train. So far, we had been on Russian trains only, with the exception being the train we travelled on from Beijing to Ulaanbaatar. The tickets for the Russian trains were slightly more expensive than a Central Asian carrier but it was definitely for the better. Both in terms of relative safety and comfort, they were the better choice. For now, we were once again hurtling onward on board a Russian sleeper train, this time bound for the Kazakhstani border.

Judging from a map at a desk, you might think that this leg of our journey wasn't that lengthy compared to say, some of the far-eastern stretches. But you'd be wrong. This section was no different in its duration, which meant it was time to drink, converse, and rest our heads yet again.

The train reached the border sometime in the morning. I remember this because I was awake and awaiting the customary border guard checks. A Russian border officer would walk the length of the train, and everyone had to remain in their bunks for the duration, so nobody slipped through the net.

I produced my passport on demand, as usual.

The guard looked down at my British passport, looked

at me, and then down at the passport again.

"Look straight ahead", she barked at me in Russian, getting slightly angry when I didn't fully understand.

She looked me up and down and stepped closer. I looked her in the eye. Again, she barked a command and I tried my best to comply.

"Where are you from?" she quizzed.

"*Velika Britannia*", I answered after a pause, still not fully conversant in Russian.

"Date of birth?"

Again, I answered.

She paused. I knew I had done no wrong, but it was good she was checking. After a longer stare, she tossed the passport back over to me rather aggressively and marched on down the carriage.

"Next!" she snapped; a hint of weariness showing in her voice.

When she had gone, I gathered from the other passengers that sometimes people with very dark profiles and foreign passports are suspected of being Chechens or otherwise from the Caucasus region, and this was most likely what the holdup was about with me. Given Russia's record with that part of the world, it paid to not be mistaken for a Chechen. I wasn't particularly dark but compared to the rest of the occupants of the train I suppose I could be taken to be a southern European at least. My hair had gotten lighter in Japan anyway, but my passport photo was a few years older, and very dark in its features. Russia's past with that area of the world was not yet dead, and apparently still had repercussions in places as remote as Kazakhstan.

As before, the train was the perfect place to witness the wonder of the Asian plains transform over a period of a few days. This time, rather than the Siberian forests or the verdant Mongolian hills, the landscape went from slushy and muddy terrain into flatter, greener fields.

The sun was setting in the west, to the right-hand side of the train as we ploughed south, and the land had become completely flat. It was only punctuated by the occasional small body of water and the endless telegraph pylons which crisscrossed the plain, bound for villages and towns beyond the horizon.

As the sun rose again the next morning, the landscape had turned a light brown and tan colour, with melancholy yellow prairie replacing the lush grassland of Russia. The new bright sun reminded me of summer. The cold stretches, the smog, and the rain of our journey were momentarily forgotten, thousands of miles of railway track between those memories and us.

It was just before breakfast time as the train groaned to a stop in Almaty's main railway station.

As Craig and I sat at the table in the station, with a cup of tea each, we got talking with two Kazakhstani soldiers. Both were of indigenous descent, which meant that they looked more Mongolian than typically Asian. They were both lean, with high cheek bones and hardened eyes. Only one spoke a little English, so we talked largely in Russian with him whilst his mate grabbed some hot drinks. He naturally took the lead and initiated the conversation with us. He came from the north of Kazakhstan, near the Russian border. He was out of uniform, sporting a black leather motorcycle jacket. We talked of our journey, and he unashamedly wanted to practise his English. I usually don't mind about these things, it's nice to talk and in this case, I was curious about his career in the military. He was a lieutenant and seemed proud that his girlfriend was a captain.

"Where are you staying in Almaty?" he inquired.

We hadn't thought about it, or even arranged a hostel. We had a backup plan though, in that Craig had a friend, Svetlana, who lived here in Almaty.

"I imagine we'll get a hostel or something" we replied.

The soldier didn't look up. He seemed satisfied enough with the answer.

"Which bus do we need to get into the city centre?" I asked as I thought that the locals would know best. We had a guide book, but it wasn't always accurate.

The soldier told us the bus number, and we double checked on our map.

"Thanks very much. Good luck with everything".

The two grabbed their military issue black bags, slung them over their shoulders, and shook our hands, all smile and cheer as they wished us luck.

It was time for them to go.

Another Kazakhstani young man came up to us as the soldiers went on their way. He spoke great English and wore a 'New York' branded baseball cap. He tugged with him a plastic suitcase on wheels. He had just returned from a period of studying abroad in the US, in one of the southern states.

He seemed a little shy to be talking to us but continued.

"What is your impression of Kazakhstan, as westerners?" he asked, after a brief, smiley introduction.

We were both familiar of the film which had come out about two years previously called Borat, which for those that haven't seen it, portrays Kazakhstan rather tongue-in-cheek, as backward, destitute, and inept.

"It's nice", I replied.

There were impressive levels of infrastructure, western shops, and a decent standard of living in Almaty.

"Yeah. There's much more to Kazakhstan than I expected", I offered.

Almost on cue, he paused and mentioned the film Borat and whether we had seen it. He chuckled, but then looked expectantly at us, like an insecure child. We had, but we also knew better than to let it influence our opinions.

We continued to talk about his experience of America.

"I enjoyed living in America, but Kazakhstan is my home" he carried on. "I'm here now, and besides, my family is too".

This was a sentiment I was growing to understand myself. I had grown up for whatever reason with a tendency to look down upon where I grew up. Before I left England, I couldn't think of anything more enticing than leaving my hometown and all its boring constituent parts, the old faces from school, the routine. Now thousands of miles from home, I could definitely appreciate this guy's outlook. I still considered myself a traveller, and always would have that wanderlust, but I knew that when I got home I would look at things in a completely different way. Travel broadens the mind, goes the adage, but it also gives tired eyes fresh perspective. The countryside of Britain, its cities too, and the people all seemed to mean more to me now.

As the brief exchange drew to a close, our acquaintance put his hat back on and made to leave. As he did so, I thought to myself. In the space of mere weeks I would be at home myself, for the first time in a long time.

**

The city of Almaty was fun to be in. I began my stay here once again, hopping down off the bus steps onto the tarmac streets of downtown Almaty, this time with a subliminal feeling of liberation.

The streets were lined with vivid green trees, pruned and glorious in the winter sun. It was early in the morning; we had to wait a couple of hours for the bus from the station as we had arrived here before dawn. A lot of the shops and cafés weren't open as Craig and I wandered around, getting our bearings and seeing what the city had to offer.

I felt scruffy; by now I had a full growth of beard which I tried to keep neat at irregular intervals rather than shave every day. I had been wearing the same clothes for weeks too, and although laundered, they were worn. I took pride in having all my things packed away into one 50 litre rucksack, but the one downside was that I didn't have that many clothes with me, or even another pair of shoes.

The two of us walked down a large avenue which we thought would lead to the centre of Almaty. On the left was a bank, with a few ATM machines along its front. We stopped to cash some traveller's cheques to last us whilst we stayed in the city. Moving on, we were looking for a hotel or a place to stay. We stopped outside a large supermarket and sipped a drink. As we prepared to move on, a few onlooking locals had come over to have a word. We could do with some directions, and some local recommendations.

"*Russki?*" they put to us; "are you Russians?"

We would usually explain that one of us was American, and the other British, albeit in Russian. These days, there is a lot of anti-American sentiment, and by explaining that there were two nationalities, we found it took the edge off for those who may have disliked the USA. Either way, maybe due to the past Soviet interference in this region, both of our nationalities seemed more favourable than being Russian.

Once they'd cleared up that we weren't indeed Russian, we gathered they knew of a guy who spoke some English and were on the phone to him before we had the time to protest. We weren't overly interested, and I for one wondered what incentive there was for them to get their bi-lingual mate along. He appeared in a moment, having apparently been in the vicinity anyway.

Handshakes, smiles, and empty questions like "how are you" were plentiful.

"*Kak deela?*"

"Great thanks. Do you know of any hostels around here,

or budget hotels?" we asked of him.

He had made an introduction of himself, which was very rapid, almost incomprehensible, and appeared to be memorised.

"None that I know of", he said, considering his answer as he spoke, slowly. He looked reasonably smart, in a buttoned up short sleeve shirt and corduroy trousers. He had three-day stubble growth, and we couldn't see his eyes due to a pair of sunglasses which he never took off. His answer was at least honest.

We had to make our excuses. The bus station was around the corner and we wanted to enquire after prices for moving on from Almaty, for when that time came. We picked up our packs and shook hands with our new acquaintances. Their smiles beamed back, and we smiled in turn as we walked away.

The city was relatively newly invested in, but with haste, and sometimes it showed. We wobbled as we walked away on recently laid paving slabs, all put down in a rush and without expertise or apparently any concrete. Despite them being a recent addition to the street, most of the sidewalk was fairly unstable and often whole paving slabs and even manhole covers, as in Mongolia, were missing. Also, as in Mongolia, taxis were pretty much any car on the road. There were official ones, a step up from the chaos of Ulaanbaatar, but any vehicle could be hailed down for a fare. You flagged them down, and then negotiated your price.

We had nowhere to go and had contacted Craig's friend Svetlana in advance to let her know we'd be in town in order to meet up and see a friendly face. We called by her apartment, which was a short taxi ride away in the suburbs.

The door swung open, and she greeted us both with a massive smile and a hug.

"Hey!"

"Long time no see!"

"Come inside, come inside! How are you? Where have you been? It's been too long!"

'Sveta' to her friends, she was of Korean descent and had a neat black bob hairstyle. She wore jeans and a baggy top, and as we sat around her kitchen table drinking tea and nibbling biscuits, she stayed on top of the household chores and kept her son, Ratmir, entertained. Her husband, Alec, was a businessman with a tailoring business. His company would manufacture suits here in Kazakhstan, but label them as being made in Turkey, which acted as a sign of quality in these parts (and drove up the price).

Alec stood tall and was quiet and gentle. Occasionally he would spring into the conversation, but mostly he would listen, thoughtful but no less engaged. Their kitchen was modest but practical, and the only other room in the apartment was a bedroom and playroom for Ratmir all rolled into one. Leading from the kitchen was a small but perfectly nice bathroom.

As it turned out, Sveta offered us a place to stay.

"You can stay if you don't mind the couch" she said, with a breezy smile, "and the kids running about".

We didn't mind one bit. It was nice to have a place to stay with a person who was genuinely interested in other cultures, who was caring, and offered us her home simply because she believed others would do the same for her if she was in our situation. The sofa we were sat on in the kitchen folded out into a bed, and it'd have to sleep the both of us top-to-toe. It was manageable, and worth it to spend time with

Sveta's family.

We talked about the time Craig had spent here in Kazakhstan and the memories Sveta and Craig shared. Sveta had worked for the US Peace Corps as a liaison, an English-speaking worker who helped out the teachers. She was entirely fluent in English and was working on her command of Italian – and getting pretty good at it too.

Sveta recommended many places for us to see whilst we stayed in Almaty. Central Panfilov Park was amongst them, a picturesque park worthy of the most developed nations. It was at first glance the same as any other 21st century park, with leafy green spaces, hot dog vendors, and dog walkers. In one respect it was different; in that the buskers and yoga posers of the west were replaced by Kazakhstani players of the Dombra, a two-stringed musical instrument which originates from Kazakhstan. In winter the park can apparently be harsh and uninviting, icy and austere. We were here in the autumn and the fair air lent itself to the atmosphere, with occasional sunny moments mixed in with the long autumnal shadows. Looking closer, there is much more under the broad exterior of this park. Smack bang in the middle of the park sits the massive Voznesensky Orthodox cathedral; both grand and imposing, as befits any structure in this position. It is cream and turquoise, and finished with gold. The domes and spires, as well as the ornate detail in the architecture were both a pleasant reminder of Kazakhstan's Soviet history and influences. This building holds the distinction of being constructed without any nails whatsoever: all the pieces of wood, the beams, and the walls of the cathedral were designed to slot into each other. This feat of engineering means the building simply supports itself.

Wander further from the centre and you'll come across the Second World War memorial, a very intimidating block of rock which commemorates the 28th Panfilov Battalion, a group of soldiers who served with distinction in protecting Moscow in 1941 and 1942. This lump of dark stone stands easily ten metres across, if not more, atop a brick platform. From this the sculpted figures of WW2 soldiers explode forward with heroism and valour, in a variety of poses. Their faces are deliberately featureless and ordinary, because as well as being a memorial to the courageous Panfilov Battalion, it also endures as a memorial to all who died in World War Two, of every army and nation.

Catching a cable car from the heart of Almaty, from Dostyk Avenue, you ascend above the city to Kok-tobe, a hill with spectacular views of the surrounding area complete with parks and grounds. Craig and I were travelling up in the afternoon, after having a quick coffee after lunch. The presence of a small Italian cafe serving freshly ground coffee and authentic Italian fare came as no surprise now; Kazakhstan was at once a paradox: both cosmopolitan and backward. The streets without paving slabs and junk bazaars clashed with the four-star restaurants and international hotels which served to remind us of how quickly Kazakhstan was moving forward into the future. It was like wandering around a half-built monopoly board: buildings, utilities, and enterprises are all surrounded by humble origins, and ever so occasionally there's the whiff of promise; the possibility of further money in the pipeline.

Catching the cable car and viewing Almaty from above, it was at once sprawled out before us, the streets tangible and close; but before long the view of the streets panned out to tiny networks of avenues and the people going about their business crawling about in the distance like ants. Eventually the view below became the sandy coloured Kok-tobe hill, a few miles out from the city centre we had ascended from. Once at the top you'll find cafes, the odd shop, and lots of games for the family, fairground games such as shooting or throwing balls. There is a circular walk around the hill which offers spectacular views in every direction underneath sturdy boughs and dappled sunshine alongside well-tended paths and flowers.

If you return towards the cable car spot, on the left-hand side is the entrance to the 'fastcoaster' – a roller-coaster ride which you control the speed of with a handbrake on the right-hand side of the cart. It seats two with no side rails at all, and the cart clings to rickety rails as it desperately winds and dips across the hilly landscape. It is exactly like any runaway minecart scene in a family adventure movie. As you hurtle down the hill, wondering whether you will regret the decision to throw yourself down it in this glorified go Kart, all of Almaty sits below, passive and oblivious.

Back at the summit of the hill I watched the sun set over the city. The unenticing smog you see in the bright of day turns to a gentler haze as the sun goes down. The scene is made all the more brooding by the twinkling lights of the urban tower blocks in amongst the orangey grey hues of the city haze; all colours which don't last long before the deep black of the night seeps back into the city to reclaim it from the bleak steppe which surrounds it.

***

Sveta and Alec, with the children's buggy in tow, strolled up the rocky hillside. Craig and I dawdled slightly behind, chatting.

"Feels good to see mountains again", I commented.

We were in the Medeu Valley just to the south east of Almaty, roughly 2000 metres above sea level. The area is on the outskirts of the Tian Shan mountains, which in turn is a part of the Himalayan region.

Although our stay in Kazakhstan had been so far relaxing and sometimes dappled in autumnal warmth even, the atmosphere on this hill was dark. The stony valley was green and fairly fertile, true enough, but the greenery was thin on the ground comprising of moss and lichen and the odd growth of grass and shrub. We had parked down the hill a way, the car park attached to the Medeu stadium which now lay below us. Medeu stadium was built before the fall of Communism and used frequently for skating and ice events under Russian rule. It was white originally, although is greying in its age and idleness in recent times. The rink is definitely fraying at the edges, weathered through time. It has been the home of many world records starting in the 1950s and continuing right through until the 1980s. However, with times changing, the last time it was used for a championship event was in 1988, for the Men's Speed Skating Championship. Since Kazakhstan gained independence in 1991, the costs of utilising the stadium were deemed too high by the new Republic's government, and so for sporting events it has stood bare ever since. However, it's not all bad: the stadium is still used in the Voice of Asia music festivals which Kazakhstan hosts annually for all Asians to come together and perform their favourite hits.

Above the stadium is the Medeu dam, built in the 1960s to protect the city and surrounding area from damaging mud slides and floods, by all accounts. It makes a great vantage point for tourists and is within easy reach of Almaty city. I stood there pretty cold, taking in the mountains and clicking away with my camera. It is a slightly melancholy place, especially with the disused ice rink below, but this area has something in its character unlike anywhere I've ever been before.

Back in the city, we had a bite to eat in an ordinary cafe, another modest meal. A stone's throw away we walked by the main bus station where city buses would leave for different destinations throughout the day. The bus station was a hub in the middle of the city, but the *marshrutkas* which went out of the city and into the country left from a different place. Walk around the corner, about as far as half of an average city block, and then through a gateway-sized gap in a corrugated iron fence, in order to find the minibus rank. The whole place was a hubbub of activity, with little stalls selling kebabs, soft drinks, and tickets. People had obviously been in to town to trade and were leaving with piles of goods in their swollen bags. It took us quite a while, asking around the place and decoding departure boards, to find a minibus going where we wanted to go, but upon asking the fare of the driver we found the price seemed reasonable enough. It was useful knowledge, as later in the trip we had planned to go out and stay in a local village where Craig had spent time seven years previously.

The dusty *marshrutka* sped away down the single carriage tarmac road, dwindling from my view and blurring into the horizon. It pushed further away from Craig and I; and even further still away from the city we had left this morning.

Klyuchi is a small village which, from the journey time and the stops we made, I estimate is maybe 20 kilometres from Almaty, away to the north-east. Craig had lived here before, seven years previously as part of a US Peace Corps education program. He had been itching to come back out here since we had arrived in Almaty and finally now, we stood about half a mile away from the village, by the side of the road.

"I can't believe I'm back here, man" he mused, in his long Californian tones. "Back in Kaz, seven years on".

I concurred.

"It is quite a place".

The surrounding fields had all been harvested by now, but the sharpness of the sky above us combined with the deep yellow of the earth still left a striking panorama, despite the absence of crops in the fields.

We walked away from the main road into the village. The houses around us seemed nice enough, spacious and rustic, if a little unkempt. We strayed from the path and walked across the fields to get through to a different part of the village. There was a natural bund line between the fields, along which the odd tree lined the field edges. Away in the distance I could just make out the wispy white outline of a dramatic mountain range – I assumed the mountains were to the south of here in Kyrgyzstan as most of Kazakhstan was flat. It was late afternoon and the trees had begun to grow slight shadows, edging out across the sun-scorched ground. It felt fantastic to be walking somewhere which was very much off-the-beaten track, with all my possessions in my trusty small rucksack, dutifully slung over my shoulder as we plodded on. This rucksack had been all over the world with me, as I'd bought it as an 18-year old before going away from home for the first time, as the number of rips and scuffs gave testament.

I stopped to take a breath of the fresh air and have a drink. We had no confirmed place to stay tonight, but Craig had friends in the village who he hoped would be at home and help us out. Soon the dusty field gave way to a rough sandy path as we came back into the outskirts of Klyuchi village. Craig recognised the area but hadn't completely got his bearings yet. It was good, I thought; rather than my companion just leading me around the village, we were both discovering it – me for the first time and he again, the second time much like a vague memory. Klyuchi village, realised as part of a *déjà vu*. His expression said it all: at a street corner or a building he remembered he would light up, and a smile of realisation would spread across his face. After, he would turn to me and explain exactly where we were, and why he remembered this place.

We stopped outside the village school. Craig had taught here back in 2001 and said the building had remained largely unchanged. It was a pretty practical looking place, angular and a faded dull colour. The whole village was very leafy and as such trees surrounded the school. It was very quiet – we hadn't seen more than one or two people yet as we meandered through the settlement.

As we entered the building the quietude was not broken. The front doors were unlocked and open. We walked the corridors looking for someone to talk to about the school, what they taught here, and perhaps more importantly about Klyuchi village itself. This place seemed a good place to find answers to such questions, but nobody was around. We continued out the back of the school, to the playing fields. Again, no-one was around. We walked back through the empty corridors. Lights were on inside and for some reason it didn't feel as deserted as it was. At last we met a teacher, a neat woman in her mid-30s with a tidy blonde hair cut and glasses on a chain around her neck. She seemed to be in a hurry to be somewhere else and walked down the corridor at quite a pace. When she stopped to enquire after us, we explained what we were doing here and she became a bit more interested, noting with particular interest that Craig had been here before.

"You're welcome to have a look around a bit further" she said casually. "I'd better get back to class now though", she added, mumbling, before walking briskly down the corridor in the direction she had just came.

We wandered back outside to the front of the school and continued further towards the centre of the village, and towards the address of Craig's friends. The road had petered-out into another dirty track some way before the school.

A stone's throw from the school, walking in the same direction as us but perhaps another 100 metres in front, was a young man – maybe in his late 20s – who turned to look at us. He wore a vest, tracksuit bottoms, and flip-flop sandals. He was unshaven, with short brown hair, and a cigarette drooping from his lips. Like many men in this part of the world he was burly and looked strong as an ox. He stopped to talk, genuinely interested in us. I didn't think we'd stood out from the crowd too much on this journey, but I guess in a village of only a few hundred, it was very obvious we weren't locals.

"Where you headed?" he asked, completely bluntly, his face not cracking an inch.

His brisk manner and masculinity reminded me of the Russian soldier I'd met on the train to Vladivostok.

We replied about having friends in the village. The usual inquisitiveness about where we were from and what we were doing carried on, amiably.

I softened to him as we chatted. I'd missed his name at the introduction, and the moment had passed to ask for it again without it being uncomfortable. The guy looked at us perceptively with his deep-set eyes, pausing briefly and dropping his cigarette into the dust. He stepped on it with his blackened flip-flops to put it out. Looking away briefly to exhale the smoke, and then back at us, he asked another question.

"How about a bite to eat?" he shrugged.

And that was how it came to pass that Craig and I were sat in this generous man's living room, whilst he prepared a large spread of food before us. There was bread, tomatoes, gherkins, lettuce, biscuits, and a bowl of sugar and some fresh tea, all rustled from nowhere with a minimum of fuss. The creaky wooden table it was all set upon had seen better days but had obviously lasted for years. It was decorated with a tablecloth, doilies and bowls, and appeared an absolute feast. We talked as we ate, and I gathered that our host was a mechanic or labourer but was out of work at the moment. He seemed casual about being unemployed, but I could see behind his shrugs and smiles that unemployment was far from ideal. He had also managed to somehow let others from the village know that he had foreign guests; and could they make it? And yes, it appeared that they could.

Three more unassuming guys entered the house, respectfully taking off their shoes as we had done when we entered and sat with us. We were on the only sofa in the room, and they took cushions on the floor. Our host was Turkish in ethnicity, although a Kazakhstani citizen. These guests were part of his extended family and did share some physical similarities. We all spoke for a while, and we thanked our host for the hospitality and enjoying this straightforward meal. After a while he put on some of his music, on a DVD player he had which was coveted in these parts. He mostly liked R 'n' B and rap from the west, and put some on for us, which made the whole scenario even odder. I looked at Craig, and noticed he too was smiling at the bizarre mix of the Kazakhstani hospitality to an American rap soundtrack. After a while he just started full-on laughing at the absurdity of it all. I joined in. And then, so did our host.

I had noticed a particular propensity amongst Central Asians to not drink water, or even much fluid of any kind that often. It had been the same in Mongolia, and now I was noticing it here in this home in Kazakhstan. The argument was this: the water probably wasn't that hygienic anyway, so most people drank only black tea with their food, and even then it wasn't much, barely a cup per meal. Commenting on it later, Craig told me had the same observation when living in Kazakhstan all those years before. He'd met those who drank only vodka with a meal, and had tea only very infrequently – and never drank water. Even stranger is the superstition surrounding cold canned drinks, things we tend to think of as the most refreshing and thirst quenching of all. Most people we had met didn't and wouldn't drink them; they thought such drinks to be counterproductive to one's health. Their logic was that the cold temperature of the liquid was harmful to your warm insides and would damage you severely. Craig had argued a few times with shop owners when he lived here before over it, even having to make promises that he'd buy the refrigerated ones on a regular basis, almost a contract, in order to get them cold. The temperature of sodas and colas seemed to be the only hindrance to their consumption however; once they were at room temperature the locals could easily entertain drinking them.

Our host had family in America and enquired about Craig's hometown. He wasn't from anywhere near unfortunately, but it was still interesting to learn about this man's relations in Pennsylvania. The level of Russian went a bit beyond mine and I couldn't understand how his family had come to be in the US. With enthusiasm he produced an envelope with their address on it, half to prove he was telling the truth, and half to see if Craig knew of the place. In attempting to read the address he demonstrated that he knew a few Roman letters; he read it phonetically out loud to us. When he finished reading he looked up expectantly at us, like a child in class. It was an interesting link from here to the US and just goes to show how connected the world is becoming.

I was initially dubious at going to this man's place, when we first met him, and as we walked up his driveway to enter his house I wondered if I'd made the right decision. But by the time he had brought out the food and tea it was clear his intentions were positive. We stayed a while into the afternoon not wishing to disrespect our host. After meeting his friends and having talked as much as we could about the music, we thought it was time to move on. I was stuffed, and overwhelmed at this man's hospitality. Through the conversation he gathered Craig had friends here in the village. And, for the final time, this gent's kindness shone through, as he offered us a lift through the village to the address of Craig's friends. A couple of his mates would join us for the short trip over too.

We piled into his old black Japanese saloon and accelerated away, causing a flurry of dust to be kicked up and subsequently spiral into the air. Inside, we all lurched to one side from the body roll as the car skidded around a corner.

Almost immediately we went from one massive display of hospitality to another.

Craig and I fiddled with the gate to the property, and walked gingerly up the gravel driveway. However, we had been spotted. As soon as the gate had opened, our hosts spilled out onto the driveway from the house, their faces wide with recognition for their old friend and teacher.

"Is it really you?! " they exclaimed.

"It isn't, is it? Craig?"

Craig reeled off their names with surprise and curiosity between plentiful hugs and kisses, matching our hosts' enthusiasm and disbelief in every respect. The mother was Svetlana, and I was introduced to Nonna and Yuliya, her teenage daughters. It was a warm welcome, with not a hint of surprise despite our quite unannounced arrival. Also in the house was Grandma, although I never caught her name.

The girls had a great command of English; although Yuliya's was slightly better, and like most people we'd met so far they were eager to practise as we tumbled through the front porch into their abode.

Dinner was like a big Italian family reunion: the table was full of food, the chat flowed freely, and the place was all elbows and arms as we passed plates and drinks, and gesticulated through stories. It felt wholesome, and after our cumulative travels was a very well received evening. The room was like something from another era, with old wallpaper, a rickety wooden dining table, and beige shades of furniture.

Like with the *babushkas* on the BAM, Svetlana served lots of sugary black tea, complete with plenty of mothering concern for us young male travellers. The food was typical Russian fare: gherkins, tomatoes, bread, sausage, all served on old crockery laid on top of doilies.

There was a spare space for Craig in a bedroom upstairs, but did I mind staying on the sofa tonight? Of course I didn't mind! I would go on to get a great night's sleep. But not before Craig and I went for a Russian *banya*. After missing out in Sludyanka, Svetlana's own *banya* in the back yard sounded like just the thing after a long day; hell, it had been a long few months. The offer to use it was the best thing I'd heard in ages.

The *banya* was a concrete construction with minimal style, over on the far side of the back garden. No wooden planks in the interior like a sauna, just a concrete lower level step to sit on, with the electric heat source in the corner.

We were bathing naked, as is the custom, and it felt as good as any Japanese *onsen*. There was one notable difference tonight though: the addition of beer instead of water on the heat. I was told in no uncertain terms that they do that here. Needless to say, this gave out a certain aroma and stung the pores. But; not unpleasant at all and like many things Russian, was just another example of something being done without half-measures. In tandem with the hazy boozy vapour, we were obviously drinking the rest of the beer in there too. Sweating so much, in such heat, those beers were getting sunk very quickly indeed.

Eventually we called it a day and went back to the main house building with a fresh set of clothes on. It was a lovely clear starry night above as we crossed the yard. We swung the squeaky door open, the kitchen dimly lit by a yellowy low-watt bulb. Svetlana and the girls were there, chatting and talking, and they turned to welcome us back in.

Their eyes turned to the table, on which sat only slightly illuminated in the shadows, one lonely bottle of vodka.

I woke up extremely dehydrated, and slumped in the middle of the sofa in the living room with a crick in my neck and strain in my calves, as the sofa was slightly too short for me. It was about 07.30 in the morning. No one else in the house had yet stirred, which was good.

I sat up straight and tried to stretch. I had had an amazing sleep after the *banya*, and I imagined I probably snored very loudly indeed. I tended to after drinking. It was a good job I was downstairs, I reflected, as I rubbed the sleep out of the corner of my eyes.

I started to shove my sleeping bag away into its sack as Yuliya popped her head around the living room door. I was dressed, thank God – the only thing making me seem like less of an unshaven hobo right now would be if I wasn't decently dressed – and at least I'd had a good wash the night before.

"Would you like some breakfast?", she asked politely.

"Yes, of course. *Spaseeba*", I answered.

"... see you through in the kitchen in a bit, then".

"*Spaseeba*", I said again, smiling.

I got through to the kitchen, where the family were milling around. The side door to the yard we'd come back in through last night was open, and about half a dozen chickens clucked about for their feed in the dirt. We were waiting on Grandma to show up. Once she hobbled in, I realised why.

Out came the sherry glasses onto the kitchen counter top, swiftly followed by the sherry bottle itself. I looked at the clock. It was 8.oo am. I hadn't had a drink in, oh, maybe six hours.

Grinning, Grandma topped all the glasses to the brim with determination, her shaky hands not spilling a single drop. Reaching over to the hob, she then proceeded to put three fried eggs dripping in oil on each of our plates.

"Do you want to know how I've lived so long?", she asked.

"Of course", said Craig, smiling at her, anticipating what was coming, "...sure".

Like most older women in these parts, I got the impression she had lived through a lot of hardship in her life.

"Start each day this way" she ventured, wagging a finger. "Three eggs, and three glasses of sherry. Gives you the constitution of an ox and the mind of a fox".

Craig and I looked at each other and raised a knowing eyebrow, both observing the attitude to alcohol. We hadn't expected any more after last night, but I guess it was part of life here and we didn't want to offend our hosts. Drinking at any time of day was socially acceptable here, as long as you paced yourself and ate with it.

I had what I could of the eggs and downed the first glass of sherry like a shot. We all took our breath after the alcohol burn on the throat, except for Grandma, who had it like it was nothing but squash, and barely even lifted her head in our direction. My blood alcohol levels had taken a hammering in Russia and Kazakhstan. Nobody had better light a match near me any time soon, I thought.

I turned to the family.

"*Sto gram, davai!*", I joked, thinking they might not get the reference.

Svetlana stopped to refill the glasses once more.

"*...Sto gram!?*", she offered, as we started to laugh.

Central Kazakhstan is a bleak place, similar in topography to Mongolia, but somehow more desolate; wearier. As a former part of the USSR, and currently an ally to the Russian Federation, the country seemed to share the same icy traits as its northerly neighbour. Almaty was bright and breezy, but I was turning north, to the border, and to cross into Russia for the second time on this trip.

The space launches by the Russians in the space race had left Earth from the enormous Baikonur Cosmodrome located in Central Kazakhstan, and Yuri Gagarin become the pioneer of Soviet space exploration from here in 1961. The Cosmodrome still stands, a testament to the Soviets previous faith in space travel and attesting further to the seriousness with which the 'space race' was regarded.

Built in 1955, the Cosmodrome still serves all Russian space missions and is leased to Russia by the Kazakhstanis until 2050. It also served as a test facility for their ballistic missiles, although it is less famous for that. A whole town (later, granted city status) was built to serve the Cosmodrome, and was named Leninsk. Presently it's called Baikonur; and coupled with the kilometres of new roads, railways, and infrastructure, the whole thing made for one of the most costly Soviet projects ever. There stands today a museum dedicated to the space programs of Soviet Russia – right next to the preserved cottage that Yuri Gagarin lived in whilst a Cosmonaut here.

Baikonur Cosmodrome is not without controversy either – the impact it has had on the surrounding steppe has been a cause for concern over the years too. Critics argue that wildlife and bird populations in the flight path of Soviet rockets suffered and died. Even humans who took part in the incineration of dead wildlife resulting from the space flights have died or caught cancer. The railway line I was on would intersect the government contractor-run piece of the Baikonur Cosmodrome railway shortly, although on this journey I would obviously plough past that junction and on through the steppe. I was on my way to Aktobe on my own, and it was odd travelling without Craig.

Craig had decided to stay in Kazakhstan a few more weeks, and I needed to press on homeward. He had friends to catch up with, and much as I disliked splitting after such a successful time on the road together, it had to be done. We resolved to meet up down the line though, and with my timings I offered to have him stay with my family in England when he arrived in Europe.

Back at Aktobe, we had met up with Sveta again.

My train out of Almaty departed at night, and of the goodbye I remember the eerie dark of the train platform, out of which both Sveta and Craig's cheery faces peered back at me.

A single "good luck!" echoed back at me as the train's hydraulics hissed into life and started to lurch along. Sveta cheered, smiling as broadly as ever, as she waved.

"See you later, man!" shouted Craig.

I did my best to shout back over the engine noise. "See you both!", I said.

"See you later Craig!"

"Thanks for the hospitality Sveta!"...

My voice trailed off as the train gathered momentum and trundled on into the night.

I slammed the train door window shut, although it was a fiddly job as it stuck slightly from rust. I walked through the corridor and found the number on my berth. I sat down in my bunk and looked around at the thin walls as the door slid shut. The four-bed berth was empty and, for the time being, I was alone.

The thump of the railway sleepers was now an established part of how I got to sleep, and I found it oddly therapeutic. I have heard since how having a steady rhythm in the background as you go to sleep helps you both fall asleep easier as well as maintain a decent night's sleep and, aside from having to wake to check that my belongings were still tied to me in the night, I agreed.

Outside the train window, I could see nothing as it was the dead of night: pitch black. However, I knew the steppe that lay just before me in the gloom had a significant back story. In fact, the arid landscape had a much darker past than the black of this late autumn night. The Soviets had implemented an irrigation and diversification program in the 1960s to try to divert water into the dusty plains of Kazakhstan, thereby creating usable, fruitful farming land from the stark wilderness they saw before them. For the first season or two, it appeared to have worked. However, the plains soon gave out and the project was left with barren results. Worse still, the rivers used to divert water across the steppe fed directly into the Aral Sea; and without their waters now flowing into it, the Aral had lost large volumes of water. Once one of the four largest lakes in the world, it is now only ten per cent of its former size, a shadow of its former self. This decline is exclusively attributed to these Soviet irrigation programs, and the decline has been near constant over the forty-or-so year period. The irrigation program has also led to climate and wildlife change, with bird populations in decline and the summers becoming hotter and dryer. Winters haven't fared any better; with local reports stating they're staying colder for longer. With the drying (and dying) of the lake, the fishing industry has also all but buckled under strain from lack of stock. This has in turn led to public health problems and unemployment. A last-ditch attempt to save the lake was initiated in 2005 when a dam was built, and by all accounts the lake's water levels are now rising again.

Two Kazakh soldiers had boarded the train after Almaty and were now in my berth too. Luckily this meant I had one double bunk to myself. I stored my backpack in the compartment below the lower bunk, but for privacy and comfort I took the top one. During the night another passenger got on, taking the bunk below me and thus sleeping on top of my bag. He got up to disembark somewhere south of the Kazakhstan/Russia border in the morning, and although I overslept and nearly missed it (I liked to get up and check on my stuff periodically), I was relieved to see my belongings still stowed underneath.

I got up and did the best I could, as usual, in the toilet/shower room at the end of the corridor. I wandered back to my room, swaying up the corridor as the train took a turn. I was dressed in shorts and a much used and abused t-shirt, and the flip flops I had picked up in China. I hadn't shaved in a long time either and felt remarkably carefree. The two soldiers were out of uniform but had their duffel bags and items of kit, and I could tell. They were speaking in a low voice, but once I had introduced myself they opened up more. We got to talking throughout that morning, although for once I was the main impetus into the conversation.

"What's up, guys?" I asked.

"Hi" they answered. "Where are you from?" they shot back after a pause, predictably.

I answered politely, and after showing willing in my limited command of Russian, we continued to talk. They told me of their life, not that I understood it all, but it was a start. They were Kazakhstani military but I never gathered what arm, or what their assignment was.

I ventured to them, "what do you like most about the country you serve?", curious as to what motivates the patriotic mind of the citizen of Kazakhstan.

"Mostly we are proud of our history; but also our prowess on horses, and at boxing. These are the things Kazakhstan is good at, and where we can lead the world" they said, without a hint of humour in their voices.

"And of course our vodka!" they continued – this time briefly cracking a smile.

They weren't wrong. It didn't take long for us to break out an early lunch; salad with vodka, and Kazakh vodka at that. Seeing as the usual stuff was enough to strip my insides, I didn't consider myself a connoisseur. We broke bread and tomatoes and, as custom dictates, the soldiers threw the cap of the vodka bottle away too to ensure it all got drunk.

Gingerly they started pouring. Looking at me, with a coy pause, they asked:

"*Sto gram*?"

With a hangover, my train pulled into Aktobe rail station.

Aktobe, sometimes still referred to by the more Slavic sounding Aktubinsk, is a pleasant city. It's the regional capital, and the epicentre for what is a very sparsely populated region of Kazakhstan. Unsurprisingly as it was all I had seen the past few days, the city is surrounded by steppe. Originally founded at the crux of the Ilek and Kargala rivers servicing a caravan route, like many Soviet cities, this one has seen a number of changes over the years. Aktubinsk was a Russian fort in the 1800s, and after the turn of the century its military roots were overtaken by industries such as an electric power station and other factories relocating here. Bolshevik revolutionaries were active here and control was wrestled over the city. Industry is now quite limited, in that it tends to rely on beef and dairy farming, although Chromium began to be mined here in the late 20th century and it has since become a hub for the energy and utilities sector.

A visitor would certainly know they're very much in Central Asia. Mosques, for example, outnumber the Russian Orthodox Christian churches, and those of a white Russian ethnicity are in a minority to the Kazakh ethnic majority.

This was only a brief stop for me. I walked from the railway station into the city centre and ended up wandering around a massive shopping centre that seemed to span both inside and outside areas. I didn't buy anything but it was good to window shop. Like the Russian Bazaars in the Far East, it was an eclectic mix of everything you never knew you needed. Hot food on sale in amongst clothing, jewellery, kitchen utensils, other tat. Nearby I encountered a mosque, which was a marvel, a beacon of white and blue painted architecture, splendid in the crisp autumn sunlight. Like Almaty, everything here was of a rich, yellowy tone and the dust got everywhere.

I passed a stern looking government building with square and well-tended gardens and flower beds to its front. I ate my lunch on the grass and soaked the atmosphere all up. Just nearby was a statue of a man atop horseback, right arm lifted aloft: mighty. Afterwards I learnt that it was a monument to a leader called Abul Khair Khan, head of a Kazakh zhuz in the 17th century. He defeated other tribal factions and in later life brought about good working relations with the Russians.

Later I carried on walking the outskirts of the city centre until things started to peter out. Conscious I had better not miss my onward train, I hailed a cab and again in my intermediate command of Russian, took it back to the station.

I settled into the familiar routine of occupying a bunk and sorting out my property and attempting to keep it secure. The train picked up speed and once again a faceless guard checked the train's tickets. His demeanour started to crack though as he saw the vodka bottles and leftover food I was sharing with my cabin-mates, the soldiers. After a few passes it became clear he wanted to join us; he started actually smiling, kept referring to the 'party', and passed our cabin often.

A little while later came the even more familiar question, tentatively offered with anticipation, as his lips curled into a smile.

"*Sto gram, davai?*"

I turned my face to the window and groaned.

For the last time on this expedition, the train docked alongside the railway station platform and I disembarked. I had hoped to get back home across Western Europe, but the funds were running dry and other than a little in my bank account, I owned only what was on my back, and so had opted to make Moscow my terminus. It did feel apt: I had crossed the greater Eurasian Continent from the land of the rising sun to one of the biggest and most northerly European cities. Using the Trans-Siberian railways, which start at Moscow, also meant there was a certain poetry to ending my journey here. And, in terms of cultural significance, you couldn't find two more spectacular cities, nor any quite so different in nearly every way as Tokyo and Moscow.

The thing that struck me first about Moscow was quite how grand the architecture is. Such splendid structures: including of course the iconic St Basil's Cathedral flanking Red Square, most people's instinctive and subconscious image of the city. I wasn't to get to St Petersburg on this trip, a place world-renowned for being a living museum, with architecture and history at every turn, but it seemed Moscow was no less pleasing to be in. The Kremlin, not just the Russian government's stronghold but a 12th century fortress in its own right, saddles right alongside the Moskva River rather nicely, offering great views from the opposite bank. Like other Russian towns I had been in, Orthodox churches dominate, and even in Russia's biggest city, the skyline was teeming with spires.

There was a chill in the air that was as yet unbroken by the winter's first snow. Late October, I thought; it couldn't be far off.

Bridges were scattered across the Moskva River pleasantly, inviting the passing pedestrian into the exploration of this wonderful city of contradictions. Crossing one such bridge, I passed a sort of 'marriage tree', a sculpture which had padlocks with couples' names written on in marker pen, supposedly locking in their young love for all eternity. Years later I saw a very similar thing in Paris.

The night life was awesome too. Moscow seemed a fashionable and modern place to be. The people in the bars and the restaurants, the ones spending lots of Russia's 'new money', their prosperity and internationalism showed in their easy confidence and their very good level of English – their linguistic ability accompanied by a thinly hidden strong opinion or two.

I walked beside another propaganda mural too, like the one in Novosibirsk, of a police officer with his arms wrapped around a child. Stencilled, bold letters in Cyrillic peeled from the concrete as they spelled out another courageous slogan of the state.

Chilly as it was, I couldn't help but want to return when it was colder, really bitterly cold, to experience the true chill that cuts right to the skeleton which one can experience in a true Russian winter. The dream of wandering a dreamy Moscow covered in snow would alas, have to wait.

On my trans-continental journey's penultimate day, I needed to take care of some admin. I used my rudimentary language skills for perhaps the last time to withdraw some sterling from a post office. Whilst I was away the design of the £20 note had changed and I remember being a bit startled by its bigger, brighter form.

What else back home had just simply changed, I wondered.

Back at my guest house, it was time to get ready for the return to 'real life'. By now my beard really was bushy and unkempt, and I was in need of some fresh clothes. I stood at the bathroom mirror at looked at the sun-browned face, sallow cheeks, and spiky beard. I had lost weight. Eating not much more than cabbage soup and dumplings most of the time and walking miles per day had made me a lot leaner, but I think healthier.

Shaving was unfortunately a protracted affair. I had an old razor and no foam, so had tried to lather up a bar of soap with mixed results. The blunt razor's metal and my scratchy efforts at a beard did not much like each other. But, with some perseverance and with only a minor cut and irritation here and there, it was done. After, I could see a difference in skin colour. Below the beard line the skin was pink and soft, my cheeks and forehead by contrast dark and replete with lines and crow's feet around my eyes. I showered thoroughly and shampooed my hair. I cut my nails. I dressed in the best condition clothes I had (this was a relative definition – believe me) and leaving my North Face jacket from Mongolia beside me turned to the rucksack on the bed.

It had seen better days. One of the straps had broken and was now just tied in place, the toggle to adjust the shoulder strap long gone in the dust of central Asia. But it had got me there, and it was mine. I pulled my remaining clothes together and threw away old underwear and t-shirts which had seen better days. I lay what was left down on the bunk and rolled the clothes up to save space and prevent more creases in transit. I fished out what was left of my wash kit and had a de-gunge and clear out. Razor, for example – now not required. I would shave again in the UK, so that could go. Nearly empty bottles of gunk, shower gel, conditioner. Ear buds. Old toothpaste tube. They could all go. I dried out what was left, barely more than a toothbrush and flannel, and again placed it neatly in the rucksack. Camera, check. Towel, check. Sleeping bag, check. I had a traditional central Asian hat and a bottle of vodka from Kazakhstan. I also had some postcards and souvenirs from China, and a few other nick nacks. My chopsticks, bought in Yokohama, also went in. Somehow, weirdly I was also carrying a biography of Vladimir Putin, in Russian, a cheesy photograph of his face on the front cover. These got put methodically inside the main compartment. I pulled the clips together and tightened the pack up. Passport, wallet, in the top flap. I went through the side pockets and got rid of any old receipts or pieces of paper I no longer needed. Lastly, I took my shoes to the bathroom and gave them a brush and clean. I had but a few things in the world, I had completely trimmed down what I had left, and it was done. I was set to go home.

This nomadic journey – this adventure – it was rapidly coming to an end. I reflected on the places I'd seen and the places I'd visited. The crazy lifestyles of the Chinese, the wintry tundra of Siberia and the Russian Far East, the Soviet legacy left behind in Central Asia. I think I was most affected though by the peoples of Mongolia and Kazakhstan and their countries of extremes: extreme isolation and extreme beauty. They are also both nations of compulsive travellers and in that respect, I would like to think I share some DNA somewhere. The cairns you see piled at the side of the roads in Kazakhstan, the Mongolian *Ovoo* mounds set up for prayer, both peoples' affinity with their horses and their limitless landscapes; these reminded me that human beings aren't made to sit still. Home is obviously a static house or building for some, but for every single one of us it is 'the road' too. The very meaning of our home therefore becomes one's journey: one to be walked, run, cycled, driven, sailed, and flown, both in real time and space as well as deeper, into the reaches of ones' own mind.

Outside the guest house down on the Moscow street, the bus to Sheremetyevo airport pulled up to the stop I was at. To get a cheap flight I had to choose an absurdly early flight time, so it was still very much dark outside. The rain was yet to grace us with its presence, but you could feel the possibility of a downpour with every passing second.

The doors opened and a fat driver with a goatee beard looked down at me nonchalantly as I got my ticket. Like Tokyo where this all began, I stepped up onto this anonymous, common bus, but now for the last time.

Although I was finally beginning my way home, in this moment that definition felt like it had been reversed. For whilst I was technically heading home, now it was 'the road' and the unpredictability and adventure of my travels which I thought of with that familiar wealth of warmth and fondness. To return to the UK to the prospect of consistency, domesticity, and routine was now to head into the unknown.

EPILOGUE

Stood on a bustling city street in central San Francisco, I saw Craig's wide white smile first, as he broke through the crowds to meet me. As in Kobe so many months before, my rucksack – the same rucksack – dangled from my right shoulder.

"Hey there, Tom" he said, confidently.

We shook hands, an overly formal gesture for two old friends such as these and moved a block or so down the street to a sports bar. Over a beer he gave me a brief history of what he'd been up to since we parted ways in England nearly a year before, and we laughed together as well as ever.

"The placement is going good", he enthused, in the curious yet familiar way Americans use adjectives as adverbs.

Craig was working towards his degree in International Relations and working for a company in down-town San Francisco was part of the degree. He looked smart; smarter than when we worked together in Tokyo. He also looked at ease, and genuinely glad to be back on home turf for a while. Like me, Craig had a restless mind, and studying for a degree later in life was just the kind of thing he lived to do. I had come to expect such endeavours of him.

Whilst Craig had been at work the past few days, I had sauntered around the city. I liked the place and its curious mix of colonial architecture, healthy Californian lifestyle, and enduring American optimism. I thought then, and still do, that I could live easily and contentedly in northern California. This is a place with a tangible quality of life, a pleasant climate, and an interesting history. It is not so American as to find European-isms overtly foreign and remains distant enough to be alluring. The people of California, as in the majority of the USA, were and remain welcoming, warm, and wholesome.

I saw the Golden Gate Bridge, walked down the famous twisting Lombard Street, and ate amongst the fresh seafood places down by the pier. I had seen various areas of the city and taken the tram, completing the ritual for the tourist. I had seen Alcatraz Island across the water, although I hadn't been across to it, and I'd hired a bicycle to drift around the city on. All in all, it had been a good few days.

I was here to complete the circle. Pacific edge to Pacific edge, the long way round, overland. I had travelled home to the UK from Tokyo, and completed the leg to Moscow overland, and I felt good about that. It was an extraordinary tale, I'd done it my way and experienced many things and the hospitality of many people. But, although Craig was already here in California, now it was time for me to complete my very own epilogue and seal off this journey before embarking on the next chapter of my life. Of course, I did not land on the east coast of North America and travel across the states overland (much as I'd have loved to). Yet, although this was only a small break and I hadn't travelled the western hemisphere overland it was still a fitting end to this odyssey; a fitting tribute to the journey I completed and the further journey I would have made had things been different.

Draining our glasses, Craig and I left the sports bar and were still chatting away as if no time had passed, and boarded a bus bound for Petaluma, a town an hour's ride north from the City. Petaluma is Craig's home town, and I would meet his Dad and the rest of his family as he'd done with mine in Oxford some months before.

And, as like so many times before, the public bus we were riding on stopped and we dismounted onto a street kerb. The only thing that would distinguish us from getting off the bus in Kobe months before and the current scene in Petaluma was that this time Craig was wearing a proper shirt from work.

Between us parting ways in Kazakhstan and my onward foray to Moscow, Craig had taken the time to see more of Europe. He stayed a week or two longer in Kazakhstan and made it to Moscow after I arrived back in the UK. From there he went to St. Petersburg, Estonia, and then on to England, Holland, and Ireland.

We met for a few days in my home-town, where I was getting back into a life in rural England I had been absent from for two years and, in all honesty, probably pining a bit too much for my travels at the time. My father's house is an old bakery about ten miles south of Oxford, and is welcoming and thoroughly charming to any guest, not least a wayward American such as Craig. It was also a perfect location for Craig to see the country from.

Sadly though, our brief meeting had to end and Craig would continue on through Europe and on to America, travelling through the States and getting back home to his own father's place on the extremely timely date of Christmas Eve, 2008.

Prior to meeting up in San Francisco, I had spent a week in Los Angeles. Travelling to California had always been something I'd wanted to do, and I jumped at the chance to see LA, Hollywood, Venice, and Santa Monica.

My time in LA was pretty whistle-stop, but I'd like to think I'd made the most of it. Santa Monica was inviting, lush under the blistering August sun and full of bikini-clad girls, roller-skaters, and a shrine to the body beautiful. As I worked further south I ended up in Venice beach where I was staying. The place was a heady mix of the alternative, the natural; the unconfined. Unfortunately for Venice, the homelessness problem was also very present.

I ate in Koreatown (or 'K-town') in LA proper, wonderful kimchi and grilled meats, all the while surrounded by the Shibuya-esque neon and restlessness I had experienced back in Japan. I had eaten Korean cuisine before, in both Korea and Japan, and this was easily as good. I was offered a ride back to Venice with a Japanese-American friend I had looked up, and I took it. It was easily ten miles away, so I was thankful.

The next few days I rented a bicycle and worked out on the beach. I loved the exuberance of LA, but it was equally hectic, and the sheer distance of the place made me think I probably couldn't settle for years here. Gorgeous and bright as it was, I couldn't help thinking that everywhere was always a car drive away.

In Petaluma, I was invited into Craig's family's home the evening before we planned to set off up north. The decor, space, and pleasant anecdotes helped me understand the nature of my travelling companion in a way I never had before. It was a nice feeling, thinking you know someone - and then being even further pleasantly surprised.

Moving upstairs, where I would sleep the one night on his bedroom carpet, I saw Craig's old room was full of posters of the local baseball teams, accolades from a sporting childhood, and pictures that offered even more glimpses of both an all-American and distinctly extraordinary life. Then, as now, I felt privileged to know him.

The next morning, we rose early.

Standing by the rental car place downtown, we were ready for another trip. Shorter and considerably less dangerous than the previous journey we had undertaken together over a number of months, it nonetheless felt good to be travelling with my companion again. We had a blue Ford automatic convertible, a basic car but a step up in the world compared to the frugal past of our forays into cattle-class train tickets and hitching lifts in Russian marshrutkas.

We were going to see the north of California, heading along the coast and aiming to get just shy of the Oregon State border to the towns of Klamath and Crescent City, where the seafood and the chowder were simply incredible. It was glorious redwood country, and a nice break from the bustle and culture of 'the Frisco'. It was only a few days away camping, but it was a fitting end to a journey which had carried us from one edge of the Pacific Ocean to the other, the long way round, in an almost aimless zig zag across Asia, Europe, and now this part of the US.

The car idled stably along the western edge of this newest continent, and in this picture both Craig and I were different people. Before we would travel unshaven, wearing old baggy clothing, and carrying every possession we owned. Now we sat in a brand new car, and appeared smart and affluent. We had seen many different views of the world during our travels, but for now the vista through the car window to our left was one of endless Ocean. Today the Pacific was living up to its namesake, the waves cresting but untroubled. Across that deep expanse lay Asia and Japan, where our journey had begun, and where I one day longed to return. It was a fitting end to this 360-degree adventure, and I found comfort in knowing that the friends I had made and left in Japan would also be looking at the same Ocean from their lives in and around the harbours of Tokyo and Yokohama.

Sat at the wheel, I slowed the car for a corner as the road turned right and took us away from the tumbling surf of the shore.

Around us the redwoods grew taller and more splendid. The dappled light which splayed down from the eaves across the car's shiny blue paint job was reflected in the pale blue of my own eyes. As the car gripped its way through the twists and turns of the road cutting its way north through the forest, Craig was moaning at me to slow down.

There was a clearing in the tree canopy for just a moment, and in that moment I glanced up over my sunglasses at the crisp Californian sky.

A trip like this takes some preparation. I had spent the time from resigning my job in the May, to leaving on this trip in the August looking at routes, likely cities to aim for, and getting visas for China, Mongolia, and Russia. Mostly this was done in the dark communal living room of my guest house, with Craig, and some other friends, with my laptop, some maps, and some *conbini* beers for good measure. The beer definitely facilitated the planning.

The first problem I had was that I would need a double-entry visa for Russia; this was by far the most difficult visa of mine to obtain. To enter Russia more than once in a certain period (three months, I think), you need to be doing so on business. Otherwise, you can gain a single-entry tourist visa, but spaced appropriately apart to re-enter the country. I wasn't sure how long I'd spend in either Russia or Kazakhstan, or even which country I wished to go to after Kazakhstan. But I needed both the option to turn north to Moscow, and the safety net of doing so if necessary.

What follows would constitute a long story, but in essence I paid about USD$200 to a Russian company who specialise in providing links to Russian customs for people such as myself who wish to enter Russia more than once on a single visa. They check you, vouch for you, and your address is then vetted by the Russian Embassy as part of the process to gain the double-entry visa. If it holds water, you gain your visa. I hadn't thought what a bearded smelly traveller with one small bag would look like at a border trying to look like they were travelling on business, but it worked. It did take about a month to complete, and the Russian Embassy is a particularly bureaucratic and sour place. On the balance of probability, for a trip like this, it was worth doing. However, if you're sticking to the main Trans-Siberian rail route entering the country once, then an established travel company will sort the correct visa for you.

The knock-on effect of all this process was that I did not have my passport on me enough of the time I had spare before departing to get my Kazakhstan visa sorted. Not long at all. In fact, the one shot I had at getting it would take two weeks to process and would involve me picking up my passport the day before I left for Kobe, should I be successful. So, it was with trepidation that I approached the Kazakhstani Embassy on my penultimate day in Tokyo.

I was friendly with the woman who worked behind the desk there, she knew about the trip as I had visited a few times during the process to understand how their system worked. 'System' is a loose term, by the way. It turns out the Kazakhstani ambassador signs the visas himself in whatever dried-up biro is lying around, on a case-by-case basis. Be prepared for this if you need a Kazakhstani visa. The woman was polite, and quirky. She smiled naughtily every time we met, like it was all a big game, and as far as I could gather she was a Japanese citizen who had lived in Kazakhstan previously. Her Russian was better than her English, but both were better than my Japanese.

"Ah! Hello again!" she said, as my entry knocked the bell attached to the door.

"Hi!" I said – probably visibly nervous about not getting the visa.

Her smile flickered, and faded. She looked down at the desk.

"Ah... yes" she mumbled. She knew me: therefore she knew about my application and we had talked about the implications of me not getting the visa, or getting it late.

"It appears your visa application hit the minister's desk on a bad day. You... didn't get it."

My face fell. I was prepared for this. It was OK, I told myself. I would simply go to the Kazakhstani Embassy in Beijing on the road... it would be OK.

... "I..." ...."uh...".... "It's OK – thank you anyway"... The words stumbled out of my mouth, like a drunk trying to leave via a doorway and tripping on the skirting board on the way out.

Her face creased into a giggle and then a cackle. I didn't immediately understand.

"I'm joking, you idiot!"

The smile returned to my face as our eyes met. The relief was so palpable you could almost touch it.

"Ha!" I laughed with her. Leisurely, she tossed me my passport across the desk.

"No way!", I enthused. "Thanks so much!"

"Actually, it was no problem in the end", she said. "He just signed it, with no questions or anything, the other day."

My thanks were profuse. I had to go and let Craig know I was still on for tomorrow.

"Good luck on your trip!" the lady called out, after me.

I barely heard the bell or the door shut behind me as I left. That could not have gone better, I thought. My visas were sorted for the trip, for the time being, and my passport was jammed up, a veritable atlas – full of grand, colourful visas.

To this day it remains the fullest passport I've ever had, and I keep it very safe. When I need a little reminder of the times I had, I run my fingers over the pages of all those foreign stamps – at least four alone at Japanese entry/exit stamps from before I left on this trip – and head back down memory lane. It is such a used passport all the golden crest on the front cover has rubbed off so it's simply maroon on both sides.

Further down my to-do list was getting tickets sorted for the first few weeks of the trip. For example, Craig and I already had tickets for the ferry crossing to China, but tickets for the train leg from Beijing to Mongolia were not being sold to foreigners who were outside of the country at the time of purchase due to the 2008 Olympics being on. These restrictions were aimed at calming the levels of tourist traffic and security problems that may arise from the Olympic burden.

Again, there were solutions. We made contact with a certain Mr Han from a Chinese tourist company working out of Beijing. He agreed to hold us back two tickets for the standard berth carriage for the Trans-Mongolian. We would pay cash to him in Beijing, on a certain date, once we were in country.

I thought it was risky. I thought it was too tentative, and too subject to change. I didn't expect Mr Han to have kept the tickets especially for us and I did expect a 'mix up' to have occurred once we went to his office, and I told Craig as much. But, as Craig implored to me, it was all we had – and the spontaneity of the trip was its strength: what did not tie us down gave us strength in flexibility. As you will have guessed, Mr Han was true to his word. What a legend. In the end the transaction was quick, effortless, and professional.

Mr Han barely remembered us when we walked in. Sat in an open plan office ten storeys up a skyscraper, he looked puzzled as we approached him.

"Can I help you?", he asked.

"We've come about the train tickets to Mongolia", we ventured.

Scratching his head as he searched the piles of paper on his desk for the tickets, but promptly finding them, Mr Han passed them over with a strained smile and a nod, rather absent mindedly, as we thanked him and made our way smiling to the lift.

Railway lines had to be reconnoitred on the map too. We left Japan with a semblance of knowledge of the Trans-Siberian, the BAM, and the principal towns we had to aim for. Neither Craig nor I took mobile phones or laptops with us, so when we got to a decent town we would use an internet cafe as a handrail. As a traveller you should be prepared to rely on train timetables and route maps as your sole reference if you have to. The *Lonely Planet* was good to have with us, and an excellent reference in the main, but one must always have a plan B for when the hotel you wanted actually closed last year, or the railway line is undergoing maintenance.

Local knowledge can never be underestimated either – several times we were pointed to the right bus route or railway station as a result of a seemingly innocuous conversation. The locals are a goldmine, and usually are so interested in the presence of the foreigner you can ask almost anything. As with all things in life, striking up conversation – especially in a foreign language – is an art form. No need to master it: but have a go.

So too, to the things I hadn't planned for. The anecdote about the toilet roll in Beijing illustrates exactly how something can so easily become an essential, before you even realise you need it. One thing I won't leave without in future is a small bag of washing powder. Double-bag things like this, to waterproof them and protect from any leakage themselves. Launderettes appeared to be a firmly western option – certainly in China although prevalent in Japan. Being able to wash your own clothes in a hotel sink or at a clean water source is not only self-satisfying in the way it adds to your independence, but it saves money on laundry costs too.

As for toilet rolls; I think the point has been laboured enough. However, whilst we're in that department – a Japanese remedy called *seirogan* is highly effective at treating your digestive system in cases where you can't handle the local food. It's extremely bitter to swallow but works a treat.

In addition, neither China not Japan had fluoride in their toothpaste, (at least, certainly whilst I was there) so again be aware of this and take some with you. A good water bottle which doesn't take up too much room is also essential, and if you can have a second, collapsible, one too, then all the better.

Bartering chips need also to be budgeted for. Do not use currency as a means of trying to ingratiate yourself with people. A popular trick in Russia that was tried on Craig and I was for someone to ask for a dollar bill, either for them as a souvenir with your name on, or for you to keep but only once they'd written their name on. Don't fall for it. If that person wants your money, they will either mug you or in some circumstances beg. In the very least, the person will see where you keep your money if you give them a dollar bill with your name or hometown written on it, in order to mug you later.

Instead, I took with me postcards of Big Ben and the Union Jack, and the odd London keyring, to give to people as souvenirs. It worked a charm. Whenever we used such souvenirs people opened up and the information gleaned from a ten-minute conversation where we parted ways giving a gift was more than worth the 50p spent on a postcard. Also extremely useful in an age of digital photography are a few printed photos of you and yours; of your home or your pets. A dozen or so photos are a great conversation starter, especially on long train journeys, as long as nothing too personal is revealed. In this way I managed to pick up a few mementos of my own on this trip; a Kazakh-style hat for instance, and on another occasion a highly complementary biography of Vladimir Putin, written in Russian. Bizarre, but memories nonetheless.

Lastly – and better people than me have said this – pack light. It's an old adage but take half the stuff and twice the money. Clothing-wise, I had three pairs of underwear and socks, three t-shirts, one pair of jeans, one pair of cargo pants, a pair of shorts, and two decent shirts for the odd evening out. I took a coat as far as Ulaanbaatar and then relied on layering up as required, as I gave my coat away. I had one pair of walking trainers and a pair of plastic shower shoes pinched from the boat to Tianjin. Add a camera, a sleeping bag, a simple bivi (I used a double sheet sewn up to use in lieu of a sheet in a dodgy hotel or as a sleeping bag in hot weather), and you were just about there. I had a padlock and a wire mesh net to secure my luggage, and a rudimentary first aid kit (plasters, bandages, savlon, and painkillers), and a wash kit and small microfibre towel. And, I still own the vessel for it all, my prized Eurohike 50 litre backpack bought in 2002. Cheap and cheerful, but it has visited more countries than a lot of people these days (and is approaching 'adulthood').

I learnt the hard way about taking twice the money and had to call in a favour via a dodgy phone line in Russia on the road, but essentially was OK. Including visas, travel costs, my last flight home, and day to day subsistence, I spent less than £1000 per month, including the odd restaurant meal and occasional hotel room.

THANKS...

... go to my mother Jan for being the editor of this book – I'm very grateful.

To Philippa at peajaykay design for helping me sort the cover sleeve out.

To Craig for being an awesome companion on the road.

And to all of my family, for being very supportive people indeed.

Printed by Amazon Italia Logistica S.r.l.
Torrazza Piemonte (TO), Italy